DISC OF THE SUN

GUERNICA WORLD EDITIONS 17

DISC OF THE SUN

Jerilyn Elise Miripol

GUERNICA
World
EDITIONS

TORONTO—BUFFALO—LANCASTER (U.K.)
2019

Michael Mirolla, editor
Cover design: Allen Jomoc Jr.
Interior layout: Jill Ronsley, suneditwrite.com
Guernica Editions Inc.
287 Templemead Drive, Hamilton (ON), Canada L6M 2Z7
2250 Military Road, Tonawanda, N.Y. 14150-6000 U.S.A.
www.guernicaeditions.com

Distributors:
University of Toronto Press Distribution,
5201 Dufferin Street, Toronto (ON), Canada M3H 5T8
Gazelle Book Services, White Cross Mills
High Town, Lancaster LA1 4XS U.K.

First edition.
Printed in Canada.

Legal Deposit—Third Quarter
Library of Congress Catalog Card Number: 2019943795
Library and Archives Canada Cataloguing in Publication
Title: Disc of the sun / Jerilyn Elise Miripol.
Names: Miripol, Jerilyn Elise, author.
Description: First edition. | Series statement: Guernica world editions ; 17 |
Poems.
Identifiers: Canadiana 20190110627 | ISBN 9781771834209 (softcover)
Classification: LCC PS3613.I76 D57 2019 | DDC 811/.6—dc23

To my dear departed husband

Professor Richard P. Van Duyne

Contents

The Blanket

The texture is smooth and cotton,
the weave is open and imperfect.
The blanket warms me with its heaviness,
its softness, its scent of sleep, leaves
and dry night-weather.
Yet, in the daytime, it is folded
into layers of neatness, distant, precise.
At night, it follows my restlessness,
shaping itself into the creases and curves of my body,
binding my arms, binding my legs,
covering my face, masklike,
separating me from the intrusion of morning,
the sun's yellow light filtering through
last night's dark green color, now vivid.
I awaken.
The changes in my body, the new fragrance,
blends with the morning's moist beginnings.
The sounds of sheet against blanket,
blanket against skin.

A Complete Mute-Light

Released from my origins,
out from the earth's clay
and into the luminous,
the blaze of changes
A terrestrial-star looking to the sky.

The presence of the uncut moon
is sharp and inward,
A complete mute-light.

The moon and sun
appear to merge.
as the earth sleeps
in a leaden shadow of deception.

A flash of the unknown,
dissolves the grim color of fear.

A particle of earth, its substance;
the sky's cloud, the amorphous;
I am here,
shaped by the vortex
of the future.

The keeper of the sky
and its meteors
regards dreams.
An earthly heaven.

Broken and glass
like the silent mourning
of the past,
shattered and seeking totality.

The luster of light,
a yellow-white glow.

The plants, their green
and abundance.
The energy.

The resistant elements,
congealed.

The hollow cast—
a statue of day without promise.

Lost Memories

I am trying to capture my past.
I dreamt that I was pushing my cart
through a grocery store
and was collecting lost memories
that I took from the shelves into my cart.

Now, I remember you;
when we first met I was smitten, enchanted;
you reminded me of oranges, melons, sweets,
dark chocolate, good wine and cheese.
Your words were delicious.

You were enchanted;
I in my capricious capes.
You said you were drawn
to my loveliness, my gentleness,
my sensitivity, my complete artistic self.
I was wearing my amber necklace,
an element of my beloved trees,
the sap from a petrified tree.

I wanted and needed you;
you wanted and needed me.
That was a lot like love,
walking around in love,
seeing objects for the first time.

In love, everything seems magical, sensual;
I picked up a leaf,
and it felt so crisp, so orange,
the tiny veins flowing through.

Sleep Is The Other Side

Sleep
is the other side.

The white leaves, caught
in my solemn dream.
I can hold them.
The leaves are patterned to my own rhythm,
my pulse is quick.
The color of leaves do not agree with summer rules.

Sleep
is the other side.

My clouds are not defined.
The shape of reality is change.
Yet they do not connect with the wind.
They are their own mutations.
The leaves and clouds
are stored in my desire,
my vision,
the beat of my heart.

Sleep
is the other side.

In The Exquisite Snow

The Lies We Say
then forget; the house is our cocoon,
you rest there
listening to the sounds of longing.
We whisper;
the water, the rain washes the blossoms as they bloom.
I will not go in winter
when the trees are naked,
when we, naked and in love,
the sweet taste of your mouth.
I am born of winter.
In the exquisite snow
I see your footsteps, mine next to yours.
You quicken my heart;
I hear the muted sounds of my heart beating.
I am not aware of it.
I blindly love you,
I need not see.
the open spaces where we engage in this thirst,
this longing;
the opening and the rhythm
of our love
burst into each other's hearts;
caress my face, let me caress your cheeks, your head,
your closed eyes, your simple smile.
I belong to you—you are always inside me,
our lips press like leaves.

Under The Yellow Tree

Under the yellow tree
the sunflowers carried over,
and the man stood, staring,
waiting, waiting,
alone and numb.
And who could speak to him
through the lime-shaded bushes?
Who could speak, breaking the silence?
He, alone, waiting, waiting,
the pain edged around and through him
as she walked past him
(he must hide, he must not be seen, he must not be found out).
But blindly, she walked,
not hearing or seeing the man who watched her, cautiously,
reflecting only darkness,
a shadow that edged somewhere around, behind
the yellow tree.
He wanted to speak, to touch,
but he just hid within the indifference
of the flowered-trees, the dead trees,
the branches, hanging, broken and thin,
wounded and ignored.
Her house was wood-stained and peeling
like her internal scars—his internal scars.
At night, he waited for the light
to illuminate her outline through her nightgown,
the outline of her in the upstairs window;
and, sometimes, the teapot would sing;
then again, her image, ghostly, reading, writing,

passing the teabag lightly through the water in the cup,
a cup so translucent
it could break into pieces and cut,
and barefoot, she could walk through the blood,
her blood—his blood;
and he, longing for a word, a gesture, a phrase, a fantasy
into the entrance of the room, the home, the woman;
a scene that would open the first door,
leading to a room, warm with color and muted lights, softly,
her outline, her nightgown,
the seasons changing with each room,
entering into the dark and, then, the illumination;
the fireplace burning away the memories,
yet holding onto the hope for a place, a soft touch,
the dark brush and comb,
connecting her hair with its length,
as he wanted to connect.
But all he could do was watch
and wait in the dark expanse of wood and tree and flower;
the moon, cool, yet sharply drawn from her shape;
he wanted to part from his internal,
and the impersonal sweats of the night.
The night-song was cold like the tree, now stark and bold,
with edges, cut, cruelly and leafless, barren.
Tomorrow, he would hide behind the yellow tree,
still unseen,
where the sunflowers carried over;
and slowly, painfully, he would starve.

The Sounds Were Distilled

She was young and reaching for the second winter-shape
of her life.

"What work will lead me out of the confined and rock-bound.
What way can I free myself
from tense and borrowed pieces of thought,
from office walls, my day prison.
What forms will I resist,
what joys can I keep or remember
after this city life, leaving no scent of leaf-trails
or the damp ground,
this captive forest, burnt down.
Soon, the snow will cover my tracks;
and I will find my way out of the dry patch, the flowerless.
I will leave the walls and sterile casts of human stones;
Still, I remember my dream-legend
of sun-shells and moon-coves,
where a pattern-of-pain formed a entrance
into Wild and Landswept-Reach.
The sounds were distilled."

The Moon-Days Of Sanford Sharpe

Your hair is of a burnt luster,
and your eyes have no silence;
they are luminous and strained.
You are a man, who,
with your dragon's sword,
cuts flowers and burns their color to ash.
You are a man, who,
with your tongue's sword,
cuts women in half.
Her laughter turns lame,
and her feelings take on your shame.
Oh, what an unsweet mutilation.

Born In A Graveled Yard

It was a rose,
born in a graveled yard,
with dogs and dung
and porches, fallen
and bottle-cracked
by men who leered
and asked for your time.
Your curled in your concrete, your tunnels,
for fear of the leering, who
grew in bushes, wild
from the seashore's sand-dust.

"Mommy, I softly picked a flower for your pleasure."

Flowers should not be grown only for the few,
so you jumped the fences, over,
and stole roses, tar-born and gravel-fed
where the men, the leering,
hid in your nights.

The Awakening

I was kidnapped.
No, my soul was stolen
while I was starving
in the deficient amniotic fluid in my mother's womb.
Perhaps, after the harsh
and false-light burst forth,
the brutality called the birth, the process, the awakening,
the cruelty awaiting my future reluctance
of days, of years.
A pawn, Oh I was, for the senseless, the disturbed, the distraught;
sickly, shapeless and deformed in the name of mother-love,
father-love.
They did not know love,
toward themselves, toward each other;
So I was the chosen recipient
of battles and bitterness,
seared with scars once visible, externalized,
but now objectified onto the baby, who breathed in only fear.
I was the excrement, the poison, bone-weary,
absorbing their embitterment.
I was not a baby, not a living thing,
not sacred as all things and creatures are sacred;
just a green plant in need of succulent food,
and shelter (now dank and shaded, isolated),
while the water seeped through the foundations, the windows,
the rotted odor,
with mold and fungus too close to my crib.
Where was a safe place? Just a safe place?
The food was acrid and the sour odor
permeated my strain toward life

and stained me with the water-damaged, encrusted walls,
corners, the hidden places of my time, here, kidnapped
and covered with plaster dust and breakage,
permeating my life's source
and warping my perceptions.
My green leaves turned brown,
sleeping in the bed of futility, my leaves, flaking and dust.
I was never formed, not fully.
I thought I had two eyes and two ears
and ten fingers and ten toes,
and my skin, soft and yielding, waiting.
But I was blindfolded;
cotton was stuffed inside my ears;
I felt no vast, centering touch, or warmth.
My walk was impeded.
I fell, often and far;
so I sought the dance,
flew through dance,
away through dance,
calling upon my spirit through dance,
away from the silence,
the sterility and the love, withdrawn.
Enslaved, imprisoned,
my kidnapped soul was hidden by them for their needs,
their control, their ownership.
They think they can own me
like they own a house;
as if the wood in the house had no life,
no tree-spirit—the oaks, the pines,
the living spirit of trees, never sleeping;
the seeding plants, surrounding the house
they think they own;
the sheltering leaf-seeds, blooming and flowering
in spite of them,

in spite of the bars they put on their windows
to keep the sun at bay.
The sun will never turn inward, against itself.
It will enter their home, their apartment, their room,
their temporary home they think they own, or rent,
and slowly, it will enter the home, carefully,
almost thoughtfully,
slowly lifting shadows off the walls,
the floors, the broken pieces, the plaster,
and then, the illumination of the child they hid
in the evening's shape.
The sun is the Priestess.
She does not sleep or blankly stare in the sky;
she heals the black-browned earth in all its beauty,
and flowers grow and color.
She is prayer. I was her prayer.
My colors are fawn and chestnut;
my eyes slant as the doe,
my legs grow long,
and I run, in grace,
toward my own spirit.
I am cast blue on the light of my skin.
I, also, connect with the sky, the earth and the doe.
My hair is long enough
like the sleek fur of my animal-self
as I enter the joyous and solemn forest,
a camouflaged creature, now, of gold-browns and green.
Do the clouds diminish the blue-green?
Or does the blue-green shape the clouds, now vivid?
My rhythm pulses deeply within
and connects with the bright, the sun,
lit like the burnt, yellowed tree
resonating to the light-warm.
I pressured the window-bars and they broke, overwhelmed

by the pounding beat of my heart,
the presence of my pulse, no longer subtle;
and I recognized the multilayered folds (golds, greens, soft
browns),
the leaves and trees in their green and burnt silence.
Searching for my displaced soul and choosing to relinquish
the book of my birth, I found my authentic birth, my soul, my self,
after unearthing the pebbles, sampling the water's reeds,
the tiny hold under a stone, a rock,
a chasm in a maple tree, gently holding webs of spiders.
But, now, I am free as a doe,
or as any woman can be.

The Measured Mind Of Antiquity

You turned from feeling
to form,
in your search for the absolute.
You are unknown to me, now defined
like your metered-lines, your concrete words.
You have become your research, bitter
with the anger of the ancients,
not your own passion, once inward.
You are forming your life's present
with last season's words.
You lost yourself
somewhere in your search for the measured mind of antiquity.

The Summer Of Fish

It was my night of beach—the water-earth.
It was my night of moon-cactus—the star.
It was my night of swimming out
into the change—the summer of fish.
The sharp outline of an earthly kiss,
preserved within a season's shell.

Birth

We relinquish the womb,
a contained isolation, moist, closed.
We are sustained by her body, full
and waiting for our struggle, out
into the shock of sudden light.
From silence to harsh sound,
from warmth to distress,
we are born, wanting.

White Curtains

The white curtains,
The swift wind blows
On fall leaves;
I chose to
Stay forever
In my abode
With built-in bookcase
Skylights,
Wood beams on the ceiling
My special place for a muse
Overlooking the natural garden,
My yard,
Often the agony
Of losing my beloved;
My tears never stop.
I have to try to stream
Out of the solemn pain.
Come back to me
Come back to me
When I saw you suffer,
I intervened;
I will never let you suffer;
I whispered in your ear,
"My sweetheart, my love,
Listen o me. LET GO
My yoga-nidra teacher
Gave me that mantra
When he was struggling
Not to leave me.

Earlier, he cried,
"I have a strong will,
I will survive,
I never want to go
Back to the halls of ivy;
I never want to interact
With another scientist.
I only want to spend
My life with you, my love,
Until we are engulfed
In the promise of age.
I remember abuse
I placed upon you;
I will not blame my father;
I was evil.
I don't want to hear this.
I truly loved you ten-years-ago.

Remember, Stratford in Canada,
I blessed you with Shakespeare,
He said.
I joined your international women,
The multiculturalism of breath and thought.
There, we traveled to the United Nations,
Because of their dream of the teaching of girls;
We traveled to Auckland, New Zealand
And met a Maori woman doctor.
In honor of your poetry, my love,
We traveled the end of England,
With rain and wind and wild-beauty;
Wordsworth and Coleridge;
Dove Cottage and Greta Hall.
You gave me dream of music and words
Dancing and Fellini

And the taping of every country.
We spoke of Monet, Baudelaire,
Sartre, Camus and Kierkegaard.
The first part of our lives,
My memory, my love,
When I was in awe of The Art Institute;
I was blinded to most of life
Except math, engineering and science.
I knew nothing of life and arts and charity.
You surrounded me
With the holy culture of the city.
I was born when I met you.
Three weeks in Paris;
Impressionists in the Dorsay Museum;
Monet's home;
You and I were Parisians.
But I could not love
Because the narrow tunnel
Beneath the ground
Was all that I was given.
But your love was so fierce,
That when I met you,
I entered the words and phrases
One-on-one
Into the hidden clue
Of Fritz Perls, Adler and my mind expanded
I was an addict,
You were the healer,
With herbs and spices
And sections of oranges.
Nigerian rice,
Chinese acupuncture
Coconut and Thai;
Suddenly, you danced

And swept the notes on the piano;
My emotions evolved.
PLEASE GOD
Breathe stronger
And taste the sweet dessert of life.

The Bird Is Predatory

The light flickers;
hostility is overshadowed by smiles,
a reflected illusion of laughter.
The child's cry mirrors secrets held by his mother.
He internalizes her messages, unspoken,.
Her signals are quick, sharp and cruel.
Quietly, the passive child appears pliable;
but his center retains anger, shaping itself,
burying the shouts in a nest, hidden with edges, cut
from dried leaves and cracked twigs.
Soon, his nest closes, sealing
in the colors, now
of faded browns and yellows;
the leaves crumble.
His mother is control, relying on not knowing
the chill of his thoughts;
she would silence his sounds, now trivialized.
A bird shrieks.
She intimately describes her child;
each detail compared
to his mother's distorted vision of perfection.
Like a mantra, she repeats her song, eroding his senses,
and diminishing his self-belief;
he shuts down; he recoils;
as long as he does not exist, she keeps hold.
There is no separation allowed;
he does not exist; he does not exist.
The reckless and violent child
also conforms to his mother's image, alive
and awake within her perception of him.

He wrings the bird's neck. She is pleased.
From her swollen breasts, her milk has been spoiled;
her poison spills throughout her tangled umbilical cord,
shaping his deformities—he is stunted.
She holds back his changes.
The child, still desperate for nourishment,
drinks only what he can;
he remains sullen or venomous.
The light burns out into ash
as the contrived pain, his eternal stress,
beats against him like a powerful wind.
The bird is predatory;
the child survives only in outline or in shadow.
The egg is open and hollow.
Pain has volume, and the sound is shrill; my ears hurt.
The child watches a bird searching while in flight;
but he is broken,
and the pieces are small and soft like feathers.

Your Name, Your Nature

Your name, your nature.
And with a fine, white chalk,
pressing a dark board's blank,
a sketch, a line,
you draw your name, your path.

Piped-Heat And Solitude

This bird without wings,
this plant without leaves,
a tree without rings,
and flowers without seeds.

Freak-animals living on a farm, seclusion.
Thatched roofs bound the committed and imprisoned,
once mammoth, now microscopic or fading, grey.
The papered-food, piped-heat and solitude
and their horns and skin shed.
Savage eyes lost their hue and stared passive, dull.
A race horse, walking low,
and a lion of fire, now feeble and shamed,
who once was exalted and rough in his time and hills.

This bird without wings,
this plant without leaves,
a tree without rings,
and flowers without seeds.

The Flight Of The Lilywisp

A land of ponds and forests
slept in the mouth of a lush
and unfound mountain.
Left over from past days
were cottages built
with the sand of stone-shells and acorns
that were lost or discarded
during their tree-mother's sleep.
Cottages were surrounded by ponds,
filled with soft or sharp-edged lilies,
some burnt with a lace of gold
or dried by the sun's heat.
Some lily pads were odd and oblong,
some were squared with scalloped ends,
some were full and rounded,
heaving with the breath and stroke of the water.
When this mountain carried
sounds of human living,
when cottages were alive with children
and soft whispers,
there lived in the pond and on each lily pad,
a woman-creature called the "lilywisp."
They were feather-high,
and their fine, night-shadowed hair
swept down their thighs
or carried them with the wind,
riding the air-tide,
or the more subtle calm of a breeze.
Though they lived within the water
and slept upon the lilies,

they were born of the air and the sky.
With each thrust of the wind,
they rose with the elements.
Once, when autumn
lost the heavy-colored beauty
of its burnt hue, the air was still;
there was no wind,
>no breeze,
>no movement.

The silence, however, went unnoticed.
The birds awakened to their calling,
the children laughed in their untiring play,
and trees relaxed their uneven branches
long enough for even one child
to climb into this nest of a new
and unconquered adventure.
But everywhere on every water-lily,
the lilywisps were dying.
Each one faded
into the shapelessness of a silence.
Without the breath of the wind,
lilywisps cannot exist;
so all but one lilywisp died:
>"Don't take me into the arms
>and expansion of your future,"
>she cried out to Death.
>"Allow me one experience;
>a presence in this electric
>and pained awakening—this life."

So this one moon-shadowed lilywisp
was spared for storms and winds;
and she rode all the tornadoes of destruction
in this forest's creation.
And from the wind, she collected the refuse of death:

a torn flower, a broken twig, round
and wood-shaped rings,
and pebbles with no future color.
With every breeze and whisper
she was transported from one pond
into the woods of another's dream.
She created her own water-lilies
from the design of her imagination.
With each wind's breath,
she left the tides of her new ponds.
The heavier the wind's sound and cycle,
the wider and more wondrous were her travels.
She collected unknown particles
into a box made from a clam's lost home.
She transformed flowers into crowns and tiaras for her hair;
and small round things were rings;
and the colored pebbles were her rings stones.
Out of the thickness of a broken branch
came the song of a wood-flute.
She hollowed out its length,
smoothed its bark
and evened down the ends.
She bored holes for its tone,
and called out to the songs of the forest, singing:
      "Flowers and water,
      music and dancing,
      Imagination.
      The songs of words
    and the rhythm of thoughts.
      I can paint the outline
    of the forest's face,
      but I cannot see the contour
      or caverns of its soul."
In the depth of the woods,

a large, gentle bird heard
the flute's song of a longing.
and understood the sound of his own element.
Most flutes sung from the reeds of the water;
but this flute rung with the tone
of his own forest's tree.
And as time entered the dusk of evening,
the lilywisp was swept into the care of a moment.
With each heave of the wind,
the bird followed this flow of night.
And when Spring finally transposed
into her Summer's sister,
and when the water passively
wound around the bend,
and when the sun shocked the flowers
with an unclouded stare,
fading the violets and the rock-prisms,
and draining dry the moist union
of animal lovers
in the midst of their passion,
the air, once again, was still—not one breeze,
            not one whisper.
Lilywisps fade and perish without the wind;
so the large, gentle bird
watched her once vibrant life
expire in a mute suffocation.
The patterns of existence
shed their lines and circles of color and heat,
as Death's cool and solid shape
embraced the nearness of a moment.
Suddenly, the bird began to sing and sing
with the power of his own flight.
He sang and sang
until his song was breathed

into her life's struggle;
and in one gasp,
the Old Wind began
the lilywisp's song of survival:
      "Flowers and water,
      music and dancing,
      Imagination."

A Sense Of October

The fields of wheat and rye are dried,
yet a flower blooms, softly.

I walked on a restless patch of October
still changing colors, and burnt;
past the sun of summer,
past the spring's hint of heat
and the wish for a birth.
I will not yet be born until winter.

I Could Hold Back My Changes

I could hold back my changes,
so like winter, counting on
repressing the summer's sun.
The sun's character is marred,
not truly pure and yellow,
but complex, threatening
to turn on itself and explode.

Winter masks the yellow-white clouds.
It shatters the sky's aura,
its wholeness with snow.
The sky is ruined.
You cannot see its entrance.

Bound To The New Seasons

By the crests of the wind's fall,
I am bound,
bound to the new seasons and the change.
I cannot keep my time held, immobile.
Time must move.
And with the wind and wakefulness,
and constant dreams of sleep,
I am bound to change with the new seasons.

Your Never Touching

In my crying,
you never warmed my cheek
with lips, full in favor,
or held in a softness, my wanting;
your never touching.

The Sky Spirit

We are the winter moon,
enveloped by night clouds, rich
with snow crystals and slumber.

We are as visible
as the mystical Solomon's Seal,
the Star of Bethlehem,
and the Light of Muhammad.
We embody the divinity of Buddha,
the trinity: Brahma, Vishnu and Shiva.
We reflect the shape and light
of Zeus, the supreme deity of ancient Greece.

We are the winter moon,
enveloped by night clouds, rich
with snow crystals and slumber.

The Horse

In this lost hour, his impact was hope.
A black horse rode,
changing the wind's course with his uncertain speed.
He embodied a silken warmth,
a mane extending, filling me,
surrounding my weakness
and releasing my past.
His speed defied the human need to number time and place.
He rode me on his bare back, so near, fused,
I could not fall down into this uneven planet
where human purposes collide and destroy.
Even the dust does not settle.
His slender legs were the power
that rode me out from this world's distance,
the bleak limits.
He sustained my vision of future's prism
as he subdued my pattern of the internal self-critic.
He rode the foam where the tide just peaks
as we left this planet bathed in the blue-white
of our last moon.
The power of his ride
left behind us the breath of Lucifer,
swollen by the earth.

The Cat

Today is the middle of the week's work.
Interestedly, waiting,
my cat locks her paw to her face
as though fastened to the moment.
My office closes late for her.
She is hungry for the challenge of affection.
The cat's eyes narrow
at the sun's implicit, direct catch.
The cat cannot hold on,
and stop,
last night's moment.
The day is sent to her.
She has to release the night's affection.

Two Half-Worlds

The song of reason
is so limiting.

So I,
the lady of two half-worlds,

dream
the song of feeling.

Phantoms

She retraced the death of her youth—herself.
Her family, like trained automatons,
smiled only with their lips.
Their rage, though depressed and deformed,
was piercing and deafening.
Her child-skull was bashed and bloodied.
She tried to forget.

Matted With Mud-Leaves

My desk was matted with mud-leaves
as I watched my windows, cracked
by ruined trees;
their full and bronzed-colored branches
were blackened and smoking with fire;
unreal shapes melted,
running thickly over my shelves;
and all was ash.
My swans of blown-glass broken,
cutting free
and scattering over the mud-leaves,
once lined
with greens and stolen autumns,
springs and summers,
their lovely lined veins,
now shrunk and faded-grey
as I lost my bloom.

Bitter

Why is she,
after so many years, past,
stung by the juices of lemons, tasted;
Still, she holds her lips down,
and her eyes slit,
for fear of seeing
more than she has seen.

I Am A Cat

I am a cat.

My eyes are clear.
They respond to sudden light.
Shadows mask the edges
as I reflect the moon.
Sharp turns and quick leaps,
silent and sullen,

I am a cat.

The Light Pulsing
Through My Large Windows

I change pens and journals
trying to find my path,
changes in mood and nature.
I try to be truthful to myself.
Who knows what is real—the unconscious mind.
I know that mind
only through the process of writing
or when I make love,
the words flow into my head
like a wave gently splashing.
I don't know all my beliefs,
ever changing according to circumstance.
I believe in a Creator, a Great Spirit,
but I cannot conjure up an image.
I feel that eternal gift
through the wood spirits in my house—
pine, teak, cherry, oak, mahogany
and the light pulsing
through my large windows
and engulfing my person,
caressing my skin,
or water in my whirlpool, pulsing
against my nakedness, massaging,
or listening to a bird singing, yearning.
It was one of those days
when I did not listen to the news
and woke up in ecstasy—
thank heaven, no nightmares.

I heard my lover moving
around the kitchen,
downstairs, making toast, the kettle whistling.
I listened to my heart beat
and felt so even and still.

I rose to the sounds of Richard.
I draped a robe over my body
and brushed my teeth, the usual morning notes,
like music.
I hummed.
He called to me
and I quickly retired to the kitchen
and joined him in our dance.
I knew that he left early for work.
I prayed that he would not have to leave town, again,
lecturing.
He is my bright star,
and I love him so deeply,
it closes around me like a loving flower-leaf.
After he leaves for work,
I walk into my medium-sized back yard
and sit at my white table, chair and umbrella,
drinking ice water from my Italian white porcelain pitcher.

Journey Into Incoherence

The sun shames me with its light.
It soothes me.
The night slowly drifts into my house,
The house of light and wood.
I look out at the stark, frozen trees, looking burnt,
The night train takes me away
From my bond with my house,
My sanctuary.
I dwell in the cold.
Removed from my support system.
Lights flicker in each house,
People wanting to control the light and the night.
I am broken,
I am made with tangled webs;
I reach through the silken threads
And try reaching out.
I am wasted,
Always trying to improve,
Reworking myself.
Pity me—hold out your hand.
I need your touch to grow and develop.
I was an orphan,
Sleeping alone in my crib.
My cries were ignored.
I was starving for touch.
My memories are burnt
Within the fire of desire;
Burning me, there is no soft touch.
I was malnourished;
Food was poison;

It destroyed my very being.
I was splitting into small pieces—
My memories erased.
I disconnected,
Like reaching for a phone that is dead.
I could not plan my future.
Time pulled me through its emptiness.
You touch me,
I tremble.

A Bird's Wing Brushes, Gently, My Cheek

We are in a dance,
separate
yet together.
Our hands touch,
then pull away.
We are involved;
we are uninvolved.
Love captures me
like a hand over a bird;
I fly in place,
I have become fearful
of flying too high
and too far.
We connect in the cold winter
when the fireplace burns the rooms warm.
We travel silently
yet connect
from room to room
from thought to thought
from feeling to feeling.
A bird's wing brushes, gently, my cheek.
I catch my tears
falling into the ashes of the fireplace.

Empathy

Sharing your sense of regard, of color
And of pain,
I grew.

Rejection

Abandoned, I withdrew
Into my child-sphere of loss.
A sun-shell, lost in the night element.

Acceptance

A time of dawn, now,
Of laughter and loving, the warmth
and a mist of words.

Fallen Idol

Your presence, strength and love
stopped, simply,
and the sky lost its patterns
and reflected light of earth colors.

The Vines Are Growing

The vines are growing
deep into the brick walls;
most are seen
but some are hidden
by brick, mortar, bush, rose, weed.

The Scent Of Flower

The scent of flower,
and the sky is a fresh, bright blue;
and you are near
and fine and loving.
The scent of flower,
and the wind curves around my hair
and you are sun-golden
and full of mercy;
your touch,
and I am falling into grace.

Silent In My Sorrow And My Joy

I am a woman,
writing silent verse and yellowed stories,
faded in cracked trunks,
hidden in indistinct attics.
My prose, not vague in tone,
is unrealized.
It speaks to no one,
sleeping restlessly in files,
on shelves,
and under books
as old, forgotten, self-pleasures.
Hear my personal message and meter:

"Let me touch, regard and awaken;
and sing with my sorrow and my joy."

She Speaks Clearly

She speaks clearly,
and her orders are curt, precise.
She rarely sleeps;
voices call out to her
from under her dreams,
yet she will not vary;
her patterns might lose the shape and the structure.
Her days are buried and busy;
she will not realize the substance of joy or laughter.
She records words like the metered-time.
The moon has no meaning
and the tides are constant and still.
The stare of water is fixed.
It will not move.

The Child In Me

The sun was steady,
and the child in me was watching
without question or movement.
I stood in the heat
not regarding the sun's intensity.
I stood simply,
as if I had been bound
to the still, sun-filled cast of light;
the cloudless statue of day.
The sun just held onto the child in me,
as I watched myself perish—a center of flame—
my watching without question or movement.

This Man, The Mountain

I walked toward the mountains;
their harshness, parched sides,
flowerless and stone-jutting bareness;
the raw and still strength.
Staying with the sun, hot on the upward climb, open,
I saw the first turn of movement,
streams flowing in their coolness;
the greens, holding in the calm.
I remained by the water, fresh from dampness.
There, I discovered bones, of a man, many-days dead,
and by the stream's side, scattered and fallen.
This Man, The Mountain.

Bits And Pieces

He collects knowledge,
bits and pieces of obscure remembrances;
all those games, those verbal
shields and swords.
He collects details;
and in his words of traps and trickery,
he calls forth your limitations,
your single stream of thoughts.
You have no answer.
You have no defense.

The Cat-Man

Silently,
he moves like a creature of soft grace
and untamed purpose.
His eyes color
and fit into your patterns of hope,
a muted luminosity.
He shapes you
with his promise of becoming,
and, soon, you breathe the same scent
of tomorrow's sphere and knowing.
Sullen, and shaped wishes,
isolation and perfection.
His wants are here, not yearning,
not turning back or inward;
just here.

I Found A Winter Shell

Swimming in a winter creek,
where the mud and season's lights
quickly harden, turning dull,
I went seeking.
I found a winter-shell and heard snow;
the birth of blizzards and a storm of ice.
I always wanted the wind and the white-silver;
the color dazed and blinded me.
It was my hope for sleep and snow-images.

Chicago—Thoughts On A Subway Train

The faces are dejected and worn;
expressions carry the climate
and burden of the city.

Chicago is electric and often ugly;
but it shares movement with color.

Daily, the thick wind of soot
mats my skin and hair;
yet the city has a sharp and piercing tremor.

The trains and cars never yield,
a deafening impatience;
yet the lake lines the crude edges,
masking the stir and the frenzy.

Part Two

We are not yet lost.
We are regarded by trees
that bear green lives.
The seeds are scattered.

Often, my body aches
with silent fear and depression.
If we destroy, it is the shape of our other self,
our pained cry for sanity,
the search for beauty, clarity and creation.

Blushed Of Joys

Old,
with faces, callow,
child-bland from quick living.
Inside the shriveled-old
or fat-young, blushed of joys,
unseen and silent
to the looking, the studying and the critical.
But O feeling so,
feeling in their own,
their bodies bursting an inner bloom.

The Miners—The Stolen Jewels

The ground, pitted
and mutilated—stolen metals, iron, coal;
organs clinically removed from the earth's original body.
I watched, as this earth, now a thin shell,
began to shatter.

Maybe The Brown-Grey

You told me about the wind's color.
But can't you see its translucence
carrying only the green
and the brown-grey
of the leaves?

You told me
that you cannot see the
mental slaughtering of children.
But listen to the sounds
from neighboring homes,
blocks, cities, countries;
child-cries and fear—
the wet brow,
the ashen face.

I hear the anguish;
I see the scars.
No bright-hour will color their translucence.
Only the brown-grey of the dead leaves
that this wind carries.

The Terrorist

Insidiously fed with love's illusion,
his anger is misdirected.
As the child of abuse,
his mind is bent.
His guns, knives and bombs
are truly the mind and body-parts
of his parents
who annihilated him with covert cruelty
named intrusion, enslavement, suppression,
humiliation, criticism and guilt—
various aspects of manipulation.
Merely the reflection of his family,
he does not exist.

The Broken Shell

A soft rain will fall;
falling against wind and time.
It will fall slowly,
a healing balm making itself present.
My hair is soaked-straight, clinging,
gently against my cheek, over my eyes
and down the nape of my neck,
so like sweat dripping downward,
downward toward my hair's length;
and the rest of my body shivers,
my hands grow cold, frost-blue as my feet;
the cold, burning throughout me.
I am a statue, frozen and stone;
the color of heat and passion
lies buried deeply within.
I cannot move, nor emote;
I cannot be heard or seen.
Feelings flow, spill;
or are they frozen beyond change?
I am forever winter—yet the seasons change,
like moods, as mercurial
as the ebb and flow of my chaotic past
and most recent present.
Will I change with the seasons?
Is it too late, beyond my time
and days of dance, song and poetry—my waiting
to be found out, unearthed,
a dormant seed, waiting,
waiting for the sun,
the clouds clearing the birth,

the bloom,
the passage.
I was touched, warm rain water
responding to the sun.
The rain, still falling,
and my blood flows out of my body.
My stone-self becomes flesh.
I am hemorrhaging as if menstruating
or preparing my own birth.
Blood pulses out of me,
soaking the earth, the grass, the roots, the seeds;
and flowers burst forth,
all species; all colors.
The dahlias burst open, vivid and primary.
The roots break through the ground's crust,
twisting, coiling around me.
Though restrained, now knowing I am not trapped
within my time, my space, my chosen place,
I must adapt as the roots, overcoming obstacles,
over and around the rocks,
under the streams,
caressing the carcasses, still in wait, decomposing;
yet the roots cross over, around and under;
they twist and change their shape, extending,
growing forward and deeper,
and sometimes returning with the flow,
yielding, yet reaching their pocket of sustenance.
My blood clears the passing streams,
the lights, sharply reflecting the call of light, of sun,
and the slight cut of the shadowed moon,
the greens, dark and blue shapes
tearing away the day to night, and again to day.
My blood, my life—one with the forest.

Morning Sounds

Light had nothing to do with my past.
My mother shunned the light
as if it was toxic.
She kept the shades down.
There was no harmony or dance of the light in our apartment.
My father would come home intermittently.
I saw him on weekends.
I feel sad that my mother developed leukemia, and died.
I want to cry when I think of her.
Cry for her lost life while, here, in the living,
and in the dying.
Open her dying soul
and let me see what made it so bleak,
so self-destructive, so sad.
Her doorway was dark, so dark, it was hidden.
The earth beneath me was not solid; I fell;
the soil crumbled.
The sun was always setting,
never lighting our window—though sometimes I saw a flash.
I dismissed it as lightning,
something that would crash through the window and burn me;
I already felt destroyed.
How could I leave home?
Where would I live?
What bells would ring for me?
I prayed to my special angel.
I did not know his name, but I still prayed to him.
"Oh gentle angel, in this ungentle place
where brutality and chaos reign, release me,

help me find an unbroken, safe, safe place
where windows always bring in the light.
Angel, help me to awaken to the morning sounds."

Drifting Into A Dream

I sleep a long time,
Drifting into a dream;
A river, and I am floating on my back.

I awaken.
It is eight o'clock in the morning.

The early morning left me—
Lost.

After I awaken,
I look forward to oatmeal, orange juice,
and decaffeinated coffee.

Because of my potent medication,
I am often forgetful.

Sleep shivers,
My heart leaps.

So says my dream.
How I emerged from my past—
centered, creative, writing, reading, teaching.

My dreams talk to me.

The Child-Savage Breaks Through
The Senseless Wandering

Her routinized existence
evolved within her room.
The night-world was a center
where the shell of the unknown
could open and expand,
entering her patterned
and well-controlled thoughts.
If that world-center
could shatter her life's rules,
her feelings might awaken
into the unknown fragments of a new birth.

Green Energy

This room was coated,
lined with flies, moths,
a green energy.
Obsessed by wounds,
I ran from the room and slammed the door,
oppressed, yet insect-free.
I heard their droning
and the hypnotic, insane sounds.
I listened to their voices, soft and recurring,
whispering in memory.
I opened just a dust-line of the door
and watched the flights in shadow,
remembering myself
hindered with green energy.
When I was a child, I casually,
with all my trust,
opened the door
to the stinging and the unbeautiful.

The Cut-Out Doll

The cut-out doll is pasted
on the window of morning.
Misshapen,
she is fashioned after human distortions,
raw as day
but with changed angles,
stylized.

I Opened Untouched Cages

Airborne,
I rode the circus plane
high in my butter-soft fun-dress.
With my lipstick and lollipops,
I opened untouched cages,
flying in circular violence
around my circus-eyes,
watching-wide
the wheels and cotton swords.

The Energy

The sun burns my love for you
my emptiness is sometimes filled,
then lost in the summer
when I am awake,
I am filled with too much life
wasting,
wasting away, nervous, the energy of a hummingbird,
quick, always moving, never resting.
That's how I see the hummingbird.
or like a burning flame,
stark and ash
I am lifting my fire-wings
into the energy.

A Haunting And Regret

The tone in the violin's cavern
was purely sung,
and alone I retraced its regret.
Sounds united
as a flute returned a high-pitched
and shrill imitation of sorrow.
It was a song of dance,
driven with movement
and flowing without conflict.
Just steps and turns of a haunting and regret.

Untitled I

Scent fills my room
with warmth, the candles, the incense,
and passion, the dance, the music.
I tell you a story with my body,
my movements shed, like wool
eaten away by the moth.
But I keep shedding,
and then, I have a new skin,
a new shape, and my shape changes.

Untitled II

My shadow peeling off
the sidewalk,
the moon held it down
for long enough.
My shadow came into her own,
she is my other.
I am also the other.
Is there a difference?
Where do I begin and she end,
or where does she begin and I end?

Mist, Dew, Fog

November 28, 2009

He tried to silence me,
Even though I turned my face away from him,
My eyes downcast, deferring to him.
He still desires me,
I demean myself,
He is not to be threatened by
The burning embers in my soul,
I am always burnt, reeling from the heat.
I try to find the cooling element,
In the forest of mist, dew, fog.
The Amazon still exists;
My love of the tundra,
My existence is ending,
I will evolve,
I will be the cool waterfall
That renewal so full and precious,
A liquid that will heal me
From the black embers
Threatening to engulf me,
Silence me.
I cover my face,
I will not embarrass him,
His image is important,
I walk several steps behind him.
That is empathy.
I will not shame him,
He needs his pride,
And I will praise him,
I, the gentle soul, can sooth him

With my soft and musical voice,
Music as lyrical as a triangle struck in a symphony.
I tell him beautiful stories, in my mesmerizing voice,
I help him to fold, to relax, to free him from chaotic stress.

My Heart Sighs

December 24, 2010

Feeling empty, like an abandoned house,
We struggled,
Each one of us finding a center
My heart sighs
When you leave me
For days, for weeks,
The beat of my heart
Almost ceases.
My eyes turn to ice,
Blinding me,
Piercing me.
You are the family I never had,
Like an orphan,
I seek a wise and loving father, and you are my protector.
You left your family, experiencing great strength.
You are my center.
My mind soars
When you are with me.
I speak of dreams
Releasing lost pain,
The shape of
Remembrance and agony,
My heart sighs.

A Golden Flower

December 24, 2010

You blossom
Like a golden flower,
Your leaves are full and abundant,
Your soil sustains you.
Your roots are not tangled,
They wrap around me
Pulling me closer,
Expressing your needs,
My needs.
I am the river
That surrounds you,
And I tend
The flowers from my seeds, now,
Pressing toward the sun,
Waiting to emerge.
Am I an orchid?
A dahlia? a rose?
Fragrant and brilliant.
My scent of a subtle perfume
Engulfs you.

Asian Dark Eyes

December 25, 2010

Green leaves,
And dark eyes,
Slanted and Asian,
Dark eyes,
The beauty of the earth,
Green leaves from trees,
Long for secret dark eyes
Of a doe,
Of a long-dark-haired
Woman with Asian eyes
Who floats throughout the forest,
Her eyes
Perceive the mist
And their secrets,
She longs for the forest, the earth,
The sudden movement
Of a bird,
With dark eyes,
Their eyes meet.
Her tender being
Belongs in the forest,
She stands by the brown trunk
Of a tree,
Its green encompasses her,
So, she is immersed
And held by the tree
That is now green and brown.

The earth,
Asian dark eyes.
She wears a long white gown,
And, barefoot, she one with the forest.

The Wind Has No Mercy

Chicago Blizzard on February 02, 2011

February 05, 2011

The snow, the white space
Sparkles with light,
After the blizzard blinded me
And devoured the streets.
And spirits engulfed in sudden death.
I heard shouting
From the cold, blank white
Swirling, crashing through windows,
The wind has no mercy,
The cars are abandoned,
The waves slip over their boundaries,
And, suddenly, silence.
No one is seen around this frozen place,
The earth, its brown-black beauty
Turned pale.
White no longer attracts me.
I can handle the stark limbs of barren trees,
Bearing up toward the freezing snow.
My house is cold,
I have lost the heat,
The cold frightened away my warm sanctuary,

I rely on a gas-powered fireplace,
As I cover myself with sweaters and blankets,
My cat cowers,
Looking for warmth
On my lap and beneath the blanket.

My Womanly Way

February 17, 2011

A cup of tea
For your pleasure,
I kneel toward your presence,
I am draped in a long, blue, embroidered Moroccan caftan.
I place the cup into your loving hands,
Cradling it, meditatively.
We kneel by the well
While visiting Marrakech.
I live to nurture you;
To serve you
In my womanly way,
An orange burst,
The sweetness on my tongue,
On your tongue.
Your lips touch mine,
And I am lost
Within the moment,
As the sand flows around my feet.
We are full of warmth
Emanating an aura from our own heat.

The Illusion Of Independence

February 28, 2011

Secret,
Hidden abuse
Nothing was left
But ash
Melancholia
Distorted vision
Loss of clarity
I broke into tiny pieces
Brain fluid,
Its composition
The sudden beep
Brain waves overcoming
The cold machine.
I lingered.
As a soft and yin woman,
Is autonomy an illusion for me?

Renewal

March 15, 2011

Cool water and rain
Immerse me
Like a baptism.
I am renewed.
The leaves are freeing themselves
From their lofty branches,
And I am moon-blessed as well.
The moon's properties
Touch me viscerally
And bless me with the choice
Of the Lunar time, day, week, month, year.
The expressive moon is softly lit,
Recalling my night-time passion,
As I shape my form into my lover.
My window
Brings forth the glow
As I watch
The subtle light shining
Across my eyes, my cheeks
And my long-brown hair.

Darkness Abates

March 21, 2011

Fear,
Mommy,
Please mommy,
A flash of light
Rescues me
Darkness abates.
There is no love;
Spiders all over my bed,
I scream,
I stomp on their tendrils
I tear apart the web.
Hallucinations
Evoking visions,
Terrified, I cry out,
Don't turn out the light!!!
I am shaking all over,
Please hold my hand, daddy,
My body
Like a stutter
That never ends.
Hold my hand, daddy,
Then, I loosen
My grip,
A moment of calm,
I sleep.

Earth, Fire, Wind And Water

April 6, 2011

Love and passion
Overwhelm
Earth, fire, wind and water.
If I die,
I will find you
In that other world,
My air sign
Catches my breath,
Foaming water,
Balanced by earth,
The intensity of fire
Burning away past pain
Where my psyche will emerge
Free and willing
Please spare me
Rebirth,
This time around,
I was trapped,
My mind broke;
And I could not
Live on my own.
Crippled,
I could not leave
The enemy of time
I am frozen
In life;
Passion is love,
Love is passion,

Press your lips on mine,
Sexuality is only one
Expression of the spirit
And the soul.
Eggs and sperm evolved
Into an accident of fate,
I could have been pregnant
And passed into homelessness
I do not take it lightly.
Emotional love is profound,
My words spill forth,
With my heart's depth.
Love is the flower bursting in my heart,
The soul is the key
To liberation.

The Sudden Rain

April 15, 2011

The day
Rips through me,
The chill, downcast
Like my solemn eyes,
Almond, Asian.
The day is cast cold,
Unforgiving;
As you are unforgiving;
I am imperfect,
Sometimes I cry
The tears mimicking this day,
The sudden rain,
A cloud, shadowing my window,
As I try so hard
To call forth the sun,
Muted, yet waiting.

In Our Journey

April 20, 2011

In our journey
Through our gate
That leads to our oak-wood door, opening
Our vulnerabilities
When we dared to love
And bond,
I was crippled,
A rose fell from the bush.
It looked stricken like
My sorrow,
My limitations,
Depleted energy,
The rose will never bloom again.
My poor life skills,
I need to garden full-blown peonies
My fragrance seduces you.
I am your healer from a different sense,
Sound, taste, touch,
Yet I was overwhelmed
By my annual bloom.
I had magical thinking,
I must accept my wound.
You are my gardener
I am your flower,
I radiate a floral scent.

His Heart

June 2, 2011

Time is hurtful;
I will never betray love.
Love is so complicated,
But I love whom I love,
Even in shadow-form,
Even after he shapes me
Into a flower, an orchid.
He may be far away,
Away from the confines
Of my sacred temple,
My house,
Even his spirit
Will be with me,
My treasure, his heart.

Roses And Food

June 2, 2011

What defines me?
Flowers,
Still hidden in the soil
Of my soul.
I choose to create.
Here
Is a pomegranate,
Fertility.
Roses and food
To feed your love,
To heal you,
To nourish you.
I pleasure you
With the sustenance
Of the soil.

I Sparkle

June 2, 2011

A beaded necklace,
A mood-stone,
Turquoise earrings,
My many colorful shawls
And flowing dresses.
All to beguile you.
I buff my nails
Until they shine
So that when you clasp my hand,
I sparkle.
My clothes express my sensuousness,
My artistry,
All for you.

I Could Not Buy Your Dreams

June 9, 2011

You entered my world,
With amazement,
Shock
You saved me,
And I,
Crippled by dependence,
Could only share
All that I am.
I could not buy your dreams,
Yet I could soothe you
With my soul,
My art,
My poetry
And my troubled books,
As I am troubled;
I emoted,
Expressed my love
And nurturing;
You gave me sanctuary,
That window
Slicing through my pain,
While I found the sun
And branches,
In my world of light.

I Serve You My Flavors

June 24, 2011

The wound is not healing,
I wait,
Drinking magical juice
To heal my heart.
I do not need pills.
I need you as you are,
Complete;
Not a fractured love
Caress my hair,
And a warming kiss
To add to my
Recipe
Of healing concoctions:
Sweet oranges,
Tangy tomatoes,
Vegetables chopped
Lovingly.
I serve you my flavors.

My Very Being Is In Peril

July 1, 2011

I must accept my fragility,
Life is ephemeral,
The wind-blown mystery
Of losing someone you love
Or the silent bloom of a rose
That will disappear like the winds
Random flow.
Some days and weeks are lost to me;
I cannot function
Within a "normal day."
My mind cracked,
And I cannot rid myself
Of this tragedy;
I have to lose my mind
To someday find it.
I also quote a mantra
Of compassion for myself,
Accepting myself
With my unwanted limitations.
We all suffer,
And, then, the next moment,
We experience joy;
The duality.
Yin and yang.
As a yin woman,
I am, myself,
Hopefully attracting
A man who loves my poetry
(Uneven dreams that flow throughout my being

And touch my soul).
I am not physically ill,
Only my very being is in peril.

In My Solitude

August 1, 2011

I was created
In the image
Of a highly-strung poet,
Maybe, Emily Dickinson.
Her soul
Gently drifted inward,
My heart beating rapidly;
When I accept her soul,
I retreat within my sacred house
Where an angel of God's presence
Fills the wood, the tree-filled house.
The trees are not dead,
They have simply morphed
Into my oak wood floors,
Doors and scented-wood tables
And chairs,
All that I share
With these spirits.
I, a solitary being,
Stunned by noise,
Overly bright lights;
My hands shake after sipping
Caffeine,
And I avoid the images of violence

In newspapers, assaults in this world.
Empathically,
I heal my love,
Through massage
Or creating comfort
In his environment,
Suppressing my needs
While feeding him my life source.
I am overwhelmed easily
And fear change
Which is inevitable.
Do not pass into the next world
Without me,
I promise to connect with you.

The Pain Lingers

August 13, 2011

A bird shrieked;
I was stunned
When I met you for the first time;
I felt your ambivalence;
Your eyes teared
With sorrow;
Your tragic past
Led to rage;
An abusive father,
A wounded mother,
Trapped
Into secrecy
With no place to go,
I entered your world
Unknowing;
But now we have peace,
Though the pain lingers.
My soft breasts fill with a milky cream,
As I prepare for nurturing,
My body
Yearns for mothering,
Yet I am not pregnant.
The milk flows
Like sperm
It wets my sheets painted with flowers.
Perhaps I am a rose,
As the bee impregnates me.
You kiss my breasts
As sweet honey touches your lips.

My Emotions Are Fluid

August 21, 2011

Reflecting on my limitations,
My sensitivity like crystal
That can break into
Little slivers of cuts,
My shared heart
Will soar, entering into your heart,
Remembrance
Irregular beats
Sounds are like a cacophony
Of bells.
When we awaken
To my sudden spells
Of emotions that are fluid.
Water should be my sign,
I ebb and flow,
And I am a mystic,
I am intuitive, mutable
And random,
Destined by my non-linear expressions
Of feelings.
My watery substance
And my heart
Can heal you.

The Water Foams

August 21, 2011

Death lingers,
The rooms are cold,
Shadows form
On my staircase,
Is death following me
Throughout my rooms
That are spiraling
Out of control?
My candles
Help me meditate
While immersed in solitude,
As I listen to the healing white noise of my whirlpool tub.
The water suddenly splashes
Tears into my eyes.
I will not be intimidated
By the dark presence
I am overwhelmed, and I desire to create, here, now!
I need more time!
Please do not penetrate me
And steal my soul.
I will hide in the mountains
Or sleep in a ravine,
I will float away
And perhaps, finally, die
Like Ophelia;
Her spirit speaks:
"Hamlet, please love me.
Take my hollow body out of the water.

Please proclaim your love,
And I will proclaim my virginal love
Though I am no more;
The water foams."

A Channeled Whelk

August 22, 2011

The sun strikes me,
I hide, as I succumb
Within my sheltered world.
Poetry seduces
My vision,
My creation.
The labyrinth of my mind
Is attuned to my art-filled walls,
And my well-placed desk.
The pens, the journal, the herbal tea,
Or the purity of water,
A delicate vessel, an Argonauta
Floating to the surface.
And an orange, bursting
With the sweetness of words.
As I walk barefoot on the cool, wooden floors
And create my vessel;
I live in a Moon Shell
Or a Channeled Whelk
Just washed up from the sea.

The Aura Of Hope

August 25, 2011

Gently,
The wave of a sunflower
Lost to the wind,
My water broke
Though it was not translucent,
But dripping red,
I lost the child
While dreaming of death.
I was the child
That was born
In an orphanage,
Time was lost,
Memories gripped my mind,
I can not recall the intensity,
Only the aura of hope.
No one adopted me,
The pain was shooting down my legs,
Each time I awakened
I would remember
A face peering at me,
Foster care was not an option,
The peeling paint,
The neglect,
A lost touch,
The walls turned black with mold,
My closet was small,
Holding just a few dresses
And three pairs of shoes;

A strand of glass beads,
Multi-colored
Wrapped around my neck,
Pebble-by-pebble long
Until it glistened.
That was my only treasure ...

Revealed

October 5, 2011

I drift,
As I visit the turret,
Attached to a Victorian house,
Of a haunted woman,
Pacing, around and around.
A shattered writer,
Whose words
Were thin,
Like tiny codes.
Her writing was never sought,
But, to me,
She was a link
Into the netherworld
Within the darkness of the Fells
Falling into Cumbria,
I felt her yearning,
My yearning
Out of the madness,
Of our troubled minds;
Another lost woman.
I wrote her words,
As she
Whispered in my ear;
She wavered,
Yet she was revealed.

My Maple-Wood Trestle Table

October 27, 2011

My maple-wood trestle table,
A place of prayer, candles and incense.
I add life
With a small, pink orchid
Placed on that smooth surface;
I meditate
On the scented candle,
Directly through the flame.
My mind eases,
My breath deepens
Into a soft flow of
Sudden visions,
Warm with primary colors,
Through my images
I send my thoughts of passion,
Sweet harmony
Where ever you are,
Where ever you go,
Through my psychic gifts,
I enter your thoughts,
As you have entered my body;
Our sacred fluids, a concoction
That enmeshes our scent.

A Reflective Gaze

October 18, 2011

My reflection,
I treasure the moment
When you pierced
Into my tenderness
With a smooth, gold band,
An expression of eternity.
We were created
Out of sand, wind
And tiny droplets
Of soft rain.
I looked into your eyes,
And within their unprotected color,
I evolved
Into a strange creature
Who found harmony with the moon.
O I was blessed;
A reflective gaze.
And we were drawn
Of muted colors
Our intensity
Was holy,
My spirit flew.
Suddenly, love
Had its purpose,
Every year,
It was refined
My eyes glazed over,
When they were suddenly opaque,

My vision was caught by the dew,
The fog,
An autumn within the Fells,
Three thousand feet high;
We stared at the window,
Overlooking the garden
In a slanted way.
In a pursuit of flowers.
Here,
Take my hand
As we explore
The mystery and complexity of our bond.
Here, I place this ring on your finger.

The Inner Life Of Heaven

October 28, 2011

You are soothed by my library,
Reading my books for
Shared insights.
The cover, the design,
The cool crisp white paper,
With bold, black symbols
Interpreted
Through volumes of
Pain, fear, love
An exotic sense of place,
Where we visit
Japan, China, Korea, India,
And many cultures
As well as dreams of heaven
Envisioned by another living soul.
I read translations
As I want to be translated
When my heart burns
With a singular flame.
Today, on your birthday,
I sing; then read
My poems of our love
Adding herbal flavors,
Cooking curried rice
And a side of eggplant
The scent of basil
And fennel,

Sesame seed and cardamom;
A book, a flower,
And a special dinner for your pleasure,
I share a poem that pursues
The inner life of heaven.

The Light, The Moon, The Earth's Center

October 31, 2011

I dwell in my imagination;
Reality is so cruel,
It can cut my soft-skin
Scarring me,
My house is large
Enough for me to
Shut-away the roses' thorns;
These roses can protect themselves
Far better than
When I am windowless.
My windows
Sweep the light
Into my naked-vision
And protect me.
When the wind
Flows through my trees,
It cannot crush me,
And it does not crash
Through my being, my house;
My windows are strong,
The light, the moon, the earth's center
Can rage,

As I suppress my pain
Where, once, it turned inward,
Against myself.
I know that I am solitary,
Sheltering myself from
The wilderness, raw
With the cruelty of predators,
A doe is crushed,
And my own doe-eyed self
Stays hidden,
Away from the fires,
That churn in the forest.

My Creations Are Experimental

November 3, 2011

I am experimental
And challenged,
Subtly, my moods swing,
I avoid the harshness of news
By listening to the radio
Or reading about the world's pain.
I am visually impaired by the sight of blood.
Or a starving child.
Violence is not an option.
I choose not to watch television,
I am enlightened by my esoteric movies
That dwell into both secret lives
And exotic cultures,
Awakening me,
Enlightening me.
I am completely beguiled by books
The scent of leather,
And the crisp paper
Leaning against my bookends,
A reproduction of the art of Monet and Renoir.
I am my lover's Yoko Ono
My creations are experimental,
A green and yellow splash of pain.

Sea-Maid

November 3, 2011

Tears,
The salt on my cheeks,
I am on a journey
Where the wind is high.

Tears,
The salt on my cheeks,
My eyes
I am your vision

I open the windows
For your satisfaction
A tender light—the rays of illusion

Our lips press
Our tongues touch
And I am beyond

And beneath
Your power;
I submit to you.

When you enter me,
I am a sea-maid,
Floating and undulating

Your body weight
Is lifted off my scales

And I have become a woman
Waiting for you,

Always waiting
For your return
You are land-locked.

Lost Children

November 14, 2011

I was lost in
The sandstorm,
When the wind was quiet,
I walked
To the nearest city
Looking for a home
Somewhere;
Maybe a caravan,
Perhaps
I have a gypsy's lifeline,
Read my palms,
Those concrete blocks,
Cold and deadly;
Living there would be
Sudden death,
The grey, the shadows
Darkly following me,
The streaked windows,
The panes, broken,
Graffiti drawn
Expressing inner pain.
There is no sun;
It is always overcast
And noisy;
I hear men
Yelling at their wives,
The clatter of broken dishes,

The slurred speech,
Beer cans cluttering the alley
As well as the yard,
Full of radon gas,
It was once a landfill,
The shriek of despair
The psychic loneliness.
Women incapable of trying
To escape their dark destiny.
Most of the children were lost.

The Loss Of Light

December 12, 2011

My life
Was overshadowed
By the constant
Raining, rushing
Into my life
Bursting
Like a luscious fruit,
An orange,
Berries,
None are bitter,
The sweetness
Like a blush,
An inner pool
Of juice,
I felt the earth change,
A climate
Of constant rain.
And loss of light.
I live in the moment,
The past is gone
The future is unknowable,
So I
Survive in the moment,
Therefore the sun will overcome
Its shadow.
The umbrellas are open;
I met an elderly man
With a limp,

We met
At a café
That was painted all white,
A sense of beauty,
Transformed
Walls, floors,
Ceilings
And the tables and chairs
Shocked me with the light
And overcame me
Even though I was saturated
With the moist,
And troubled clouds
Bursting, wet with rain,
That hid the sun.
The man and I bonded
With our dream
Of light.

The Invisible Woman

December 24, 2011

This sweet woman
A victim of poverty,
No market for healthy foods;
Where are the fresh fruits,
The vegetables, the whole wheat grains.
Just take-away,
Deep fried,
Her arteries will never be the same,
No hospital,
She struggles, denying her tubercular cough,
Finally
An emergency room,
She is ignored
Because she has shed
The white light;
She is barren
With coffee-colored skin,
Her teeth are rotted.
She can die of infection,
She barely reads
She cannot reach for the hope
And world of books.
There is no store,
No literacy
A deadly school.
She lives in a slum
Among the shadows,
Of black mold,

Her tiny room,
Is windowless.
Where is the art
The concern
The love
She is lost in this system
That rewards wealth.
Drugs,
The glue that binds her
While she struggles,
Attempting to find her place
In this vast, cold country.
Oh, what brutality
Feeds the senselessness
Of her state of being.

The Sacred Shiva

December 24, 2011

I was twice born;
I was fated
To put my finger in holy water
And touch your brow,
Above your eyes.
A third and sacred eye;
To heal you.
My femininity
Is as intense
As my sacred madness,
I vow
To press my lips to yours,
And hold you into my heart.

I Am An Outsider

December 29, 2011

The sudden rain,
Falls on my red supple shawl;
I dress
With flowing
Long red and fawn skirts
And serious subtle shoes
No one has ever worn.
I make my own jewelry,
And I wear turquoise dangling earrings,
A hint of pearls
That dazzles and shines.
I am an outsider
In my uniqueness.
However, sadly,
I reflect
On my calling;
I am an outsider;
I dwell in a special house,
Designed by me.
It, too, is unique.
I, now, play the dulcimer,
Evoking music of another time.
I have a strange profession
Chosen with an alternative
Education.
I have the wrong credentials.
I am an outsider
Standing in the dew, the fog, the rain.
I cannot open the door with ease.

Herbs And Parsnips

My battle with pneumonia
January 6, 2012

Virgin flowered sheets,
An intimate place to dream
Of lost nights
And shattered days,
My soft pink lips are parched.
A loss of fluids.
I am told to drink
The waters that heal
All my inner wounds;
Bacteria floats
Throughout my ravaged self.
I cry out;
Who will hear me?
I am separate and alone.
The tiredness
Binds me like
The unkempt quilt,
That falls silently
Down the left side,
Flowing and ruining my asymmetrical mattress
And brushing the rose, rounded rug.
I try to accept the inevitable.
My lover closes the door,
Seeking herbs and parsnips
Onions and okra.
My evening soup,

Warm flavors,
Sift throughout my bloodstream.
I have to protect him
From my loss of ease,
My turmoil,
My ribs hurt
As I cough away the poison.

A Tea Ceremony

January 7, 2012

We practice
Our own tea-ceremony,
I pour his tea in his cup,
And he returns the favor.
Sipping tea,
A gentle meditation,
Like staring at a candle-flame
That soothes me.
I inhale the incense,
The potent healer,
My senses are acute
After purging
The indifference of the past,
And accepting the new day,
A new promise,
We sit on my patio
Where the sun blesses us
With its intense warmth.
I am protected by a beautiful house,
That shares an intimate harmony, and secret gifts.

Our fireplace is smoldering,
The flame pierces my vision;
It is more powerful than my subtle candle.
The energy that soothes like a Chardonnay or
A Riesling,
A slight altering of perception,
Only one glass to celebrate our sensitivities to the inner world,
Like the tea, immersed with a slight caffeine,
That does not make my hands shake,
And does not create the substance
Of root vegetables and strong herbs
That would inflame my nerves.

I Dwell, Only In My House

January 7, 2012

I dwell, only in my house,
Watering my ten plants
That bloom
In my sunroom.
I wind my grandfather clock,
That chimes like a meditation.
My music,
Delicate Chopin's "Nocturnes" and
Elgar's "The Cello Concerto,"
Deeply haunting, I wilt.
I breathe throughout my being,
Feeling each breath as I count
The seconds
Pressing against my lungs,
The depth, the pull,
The expansion
Of my chest;
The fireplace warms
The intimate place in my
Rhythmic beating heart.
My large windows,
Shaping my shadows away,
The light is silent
Yet potent.
The trees,
Sharing their lives with me,
As I cherish the oak-wood floors and doors.
Books, spilling their insightful words,

Expressing a multitude of passion and enlightenment.
The built-in bookcases
Reaching upward toward the vaulted ceiling
Like a sudden red-winged bird.
My ten rooms,
A spacious heaven,
With tables and desks,
All from an exotic forest,
The older trees were spared,
Their environment, though succulent,
Is green and filled with plenty.
My wood beam-ceiling lingers over my bedroom,
And skylights of slit-light shape my morning dreams.

Healing The Artist

January 7, 2012

I have overcome
My tremors and
The illness in my mind,
With substances
Intermingled with miracles.
I live at the right time
Where my brain chemistry is balanced;
Removing my singular illness.
Of crippling melancholy and intense moods, now,
Are erased by my own struggles
Toward health.
Like my body,
I have to strengthen my immune system
Which falters
With a rare disease
I inherited from my tragic
And lost mother.
I have worked, diligently,
To capture my life-skills.
I can drive a car with ease,
Though I have difficulty with maps and movement.
I am spatially challenged.
I, also, found my calling;
I heal people with my arts-therapy,
And I write
Words that confound me,
As I discover my own unrecognized self.
I played two instruments

But now, I intuitively,
Dream of music with my dulcimer,
My fingers are raw, a slight side effect;
However, my soul feels warm and tender
As I recall the songs that breathed brightly within me.
I designed my inner and outer sanctuary
With my gift of vision,
Paintings shaped into the wall.
I, also, have an intimate love,
A partner who soothes my heart,
And shares his sudden perceptions
Awakening my creativity.
We travel, searching secluded sights that are enriching
And sensuous.
I steam vegetables
As well as stir-fry the potent ingredients,
Spices and herbs.
My poor, lost mother,
Who did not have a life,
But she had her dream world;
God, why did you not save her!

The Healing Music

January 8, 2012

I spoke
To the angel, Gabriel
When I was child,
Abused,
Exploited,
The chaos
And intense violence,
Leaking poisonous food,
Undernourished,
And unprotected
From the unspoken rage,
From verbal violence,
Neglect,
And physical abuse;
Male hands crushed me
And struck me
My wounded mother ignored me,
And begged me to stay ignorant
And belong only to her.
The pain was beyond endurance.
I, then, psychotic,
Lived within my own bubble,
Dancing and inner music,
The chimes
Like a metronome ticking away my virgin life.
I tried to give birth to myself;
The sun mocked me,
So, I chose the moon.

And spoke to the soft light;
A treasure only I received,
There I was,
In a silent haze
Waiting for Gabriel to release me.
The flute and the dulcimer
Heal me with the tremors of music.

All His Love Was Wasted Away

January 9, 2012

He destroyed
Most of my life,
However,
I have feelings of confusion, almost empathy
For his complex illness.
He swallowed
Words of love,
Words of praise.
I was born,
Entering a
Room, mad with convulsions and
Frightening eruptions.
He pinned me against the closed door,
He crushed me,
I cried out,
But he just laughed and laughed.
He tormented me;
I wished he would leave us.
A keening,
A child born to absorb
The ugly words
That pressed against his teeth.
Could he control his abuse?
He was damaged;
His mother struck him with a stick,
Over and over again
Until his feelings died.
His weapon was rage
And inflicting pain.
All his love

Was wasted away,
Like a living corpse.
Now that he is very old,
I feel pity and sorrow
For his self-destructive life.
I, still, want to nourish him.
As I feel released
From my still-born birth.

I Create Intimacy

January 13, 2012

I steamed broccoli
With Swiss cheese
Over rice
Adding exotic spices.
Tonight,
I am serving succotash;
The ground black pepper
Tears my eyes.
But I have no sorrow
That is served and breaded in my meals.
My endorphins rise
Like a loaf of sourdough bread,
Like a meditation,
My thoughts
Are spared from the darkness,
Which intrudes the other side of my soul.
I sing,
As I sift flour;
A melodious nightingale,
Is intrigued
Outside my window
On a snow-topped branch
Singing his nocturnal song.
The flora,
The fauna,
Both claim my bow windows,
Where my plants breathe,
As I create intimacy;

There is no heartbreak
Blending the source of my love
With fresh chopped basil.

Replenishing

January 16, 2012

Occluding foliage
Brushes against
My white, muslin dress,
The silence,
The roots of a Ginkgo tree
Are not poisonous.
I have no fear.
Yellow jackets return
In the year's subtle spring,
Yet,
I pour honey
Into my Jasmine tea
In the winter-season.
The Fir trees
Always bloom
Into a dark green,
Replenishing my
Fallow ground,
Small,
Yet significant.
I was born in winter,
So I seek flowers that thrive
In the shadows,
They are in harmony
With my own senses.

Mood Swings

January 17, 2012

My moods
Float on the waves of the sea.
Sometimes,
The waves are calm
Sometimes,
The waves are frighteningly high,
Shifting
Like a whirlwind,
Or a squall.
Waiting for me to drown,
Lake-moods
Shatter ships,
I rescue the innocents
Struggling in the water
I am swallowing
Gulps of seaweed or kelp
Breathing intermittently,
Waves, too powerful
To contain.
My essence is water,
The fluid fills my lungs,
However,
I am revived
By the sharp figure-in-the-shadows
Who owns the lighthouse,
I will always be waiting
For the unpredictable wave
To change its course.

Sudden Embraces

January 24, 2012

Snow plowed streets
Small drifts,
Ice shattering my ease.
Flowers and stems,
The roots are deeply imbedded
In the tired ground.
Throughout this season
I am embraced
By winter,
Almost suffocating me,
Coated with feather-like snow,
They float down to reach me,
Like you reach me,
Sudden embraces
Increase my fragility,
Yet warm me;
I want to be held,
As the ice melts.

A Separate Journey

January 19, 2012

He did not know me;
My calling was complete
With long cotton dresses,
Not silk.
My room was small
My slant of vision
The light
Flashing black and white images.
Prolific in words and songs,
The strings of my dulcimer
And my precious ivory keys
Did not move him,
A chill,
I wrote from
A deep place, not hollow
Which thwarted his love;
He would not listen.
The leather bindings of books,
Their essence
Of longing and love
That purified my spirit.
He was bursting with envy
For money and mansions,
Where the gardens
Are filled with weeds
His path was impeded
By my very existence.
He chose
A separate journey.

Burgundy Wine

January 31, 2012

She disappeared
From my life
Persimmons and pepper
Mixed with exotic spices
Was her only joy.
I would sigh
Perceiving the lush colors
Of a wild salad.
Her life
Was as empty
As a wine-glass,
Ignoring
The color of burgundy,
Celebratory,
An affirmation of life.
She would dream
Of vanished worlds
Or clues hidden in her books.
Her imagination
Floated within the clouds,
And the moon.
I could not grasp her hand,
She could not hold me,
My skin, still dry,
Peeling,
Where was her precious touch?
She was numb,
Living in a toxic maze,

That hid her
With no hope for an exit.
She retreated into
And was surrounded
By the purity of glass
Where there is no sliver.
My eyes adjusted
To her invisibility
She loved luscious images
Of art,
The creation of beauty.
The lines, the shadows,
The sun-leaves,
A moment in time,
Silently captured,
She wrapped herself
In a tea-gown,
Sometimes a caftan,
Living only for the moment;
Her platelets,
Her bone scans,
Released her
From life's pain.
Mommy, I miss you.

Flutes And Dulcimers

February 18, 2012

I bloom
With my plants,
The roots
Are bound.
Yet they flourish within
Terra cotta and ceramic vessels,
Leaf by leaf,
Always a green
And vibrant birth,
They quiver
To the surrounding music,
Flutes and dulcimers
Resolve into winter-blossoms.
Rejuvenation,
And mortal incandescence.
Their pulsing energy
Ignites my visceral flame
Like a secret white-red candle,
A subtle glow
Scented with lilacs,
The abundance of a deep-rooted bouquet,
Our love.

A Splash Of Green

March 15, 2012

Pain is the color of the sun,
And burnt embers,
They have no shadow,
Sun spills light;
While my skin burns,
Overly bright,
I half-close my eyes
While I dwell in the day,
My skin is sensitized,
The warm shades of the earth,
Brown, black and ember
A splash of green
From my ginkgo tree,
The sod, the grass,
Flowers the shape of their colors
As they unfold
Pointed, round, bare as a tulip.
The bees know;
They never sting me.

Fetishes And A Talisman

March 22, 2012

My dreams and pursuits,
Are poisoned; I succumbed.
I cannot rid myself of stress
And the variations on that theme.
I shun life as it is,
I will become a humble potter,
Feeling the soft/hard loam beneath my nails.
Around and around like a meditation,
Soothing and rhythmic.
I, now, escape.
Native American drumming
And prayer,
Fetishes and a talisman.

Sacred Water

March 31, 2012

The rings of Saturn,
The death of a star,
And, then, its birth,
I succumb to the light
Of ancient readings,
The constellation that forms Aquarius.
Though my essence is air,
I seek the ocean;
I bear birth to water;
A baby is born after
The water breaks,
Symbiosis—the sacred mother
And her child.
The fetus
Swims
Revealing gills;
The nature of fish,
And, then
The afterbirth;
Swimming upstream
The semen dwells
Within her home,
Her womb.

A Crisis Of Faith

March 25, 2012

I cannot conceive
Of the existential angst
Of nothingness.
My soul
Permeates me,
My tenement is my body
Until my coming reincarnation,
Or the cloud-filled
Translation of heaven,
Transformed
Into a subtle mist,
Floating and bonding
Seeking other-worldly apparitions;
I prepare
The substance of seeds
And the bursting of flowers
And rooted trees,
I am an animist.

Transformation

April 4, 2012
It Is Hard to Trust Your Love of Another,
when One Has a History of Feeling Unloved.
—Allan Bruce Zee

Bitter fruit,
Pomegranates spoiled
Oranges decay,
Tomato is a fruit,
Cut thinly
With my mandolin,
The blade,
Slicing and shredding.
Abundance surrounds me,
Look to the trees
Their fruit, bursting
With health,
Unimpaired,
The tree nurtures
Its bounty,
Then, this fruit, now ripe,
Ruddy and plump,
Graces my wicker basket
As I ingest
And transform its energy.

The Surface Of My Mind

April 9, 2012
So oft have I invoked thee for my Muse
—William Shakespeare, *Sonnet 78*

I am obtuse
In the truest of my love,
I expire
As I covet
Your distinct words,
I cherish
The fullness
Of you
Which differs
From the surface of my mind.
I am ruined
By the quest for love,
Shadows
From my elapsed birth,
My bond breaks
The seemingly unbroken glass,
I am daring
Though I may be shattered;
The scars are masked
Though images appear
Throughout my dreams,
As well as spirits
Reveal an interior spark.

I Give Alms

April 26, 2012

I seek,
And tremble,
Seated under
The refuge
Of a yellowed-leaf
And silent,
Though, often, rustling
Eucalyptus tree;
Parchment and grainy,
Its leaves fall
Like whispers.
The sky explodes into a white light;
My eyes tear with awe.
I give alms,
Of spare water,
Indulging the roots
With subsistence.
My newly washed
Long, pine-colored dress,
Caught on a low branch,
This tree desires my intimacy.

The Beat Of My Heart

May 7, 2012

The chimes
Of my grandfather clock,
The intentional rhythm;
I wind an aspect of its surface.
The burnished oak wood
Paints a luster of visual and grainy senses.
The distillation
Of lost minutes,
A distant conversation,
That blends
Both the rhythm and the music,
Which sings the harmony
That pulses
To the beat of my heart.

The Scent Of Heaven

May 7, 2012

Light sheds color,
My dream is dusk.
The pattern and texture
Of my skin
Small, moist pores
Still breathe in the fragrance
Of dawn,
The golden moon
Glides along with me
To the end of time,
The scent of heaven.
Where tulips never wilt,
They are never shapeless,
And they blush in the rainbow,
Over the hue
Of clouds.

White Pearls

May 8, 2012

Time is the source that caresses me during my lingering days
My meditation
Reaches into my father's arms,
He, also, wanted me in his bed.
I simply remember the sheets and towels.
He no longer desired my mother.
Now, I feel his incredible peace.
An emotion of white pearls
Sliding across my breasts.
Now, he is free from sorrow and psychic pain
He, too, was abused by parents
Who were damaged by the pogroms of Kiev.
The poverty, the horror of genocide of an entire people.
They survived in pieces;
And had no range of knowledge;
Children were meant to be abused,
As their family before them
And the family beyond them.
There is no bigotry beyond the realm.
I am too numbed by my mind swirling and overwhelmed.
It is too painful to feel.
Maybe I, too, will be free from psychic pain.

Burnt Offerings

May 14, 2012

Psychic wounds,
My fears are like open wounds
Without scabs, never healing.
I am caught in the web
Bound,
Searched and devoured.
One more cut,
My bleeding until death
Releases me
From my terror.
Words, assaulting
Like poison,
Syrupy, its overly sweet substance
Churning in my being,
Then and now,
Burnt offerings,
Words turn into ashes.

Solitude Haunts Me

May 31, 2012

Sadly,
I miss you,
Your face,
Your love,
Your longing.
I will not sever our coupling.
I await your presence,
Solitude haunts me,
The pain, sheltering
My core-self
My hair is wet
With the storm.
The shadowed clouds
Reappear
When I am unaware
And unsound.
I crave mountains
That turn green from translucent streams.
The wind, pressed
Against my desire,
My tattered dreams,
Ephemeral,
My swollen eyes,
Tenacious tears
Like a waterfall,
My vision is impaired.

The Center Of The Day

June 11, 2012

Disabled,
I sleep
Through the
Center of the day;
Longing
To be sand-beige,
Blending into society,
The fluid in my mind,
Drips unevenly
I fall,
Blood leaks throughout my body
Towards the cut,
Violating me
Yet cleansing me like menstruation.
My energy fails,
Solitude,
My peaceful room
Light, reflecting and uneven,
The sun mocks me.
Psychic pain
Will never release me
From my vital fluid,
Uncongealed.

Twilight

June 11, 2012

Twilight,
The time we met,
The colors of a prism,
The trees
Of blended shadows
And color,
The red
And yellow leaf
Shaped itself,
On my scented chestnut hair,
My perfume rose into
My burnished wind-soaked tresses.
The leaves
Were solidly connected
With their tremulous bark.
I felt wings crush against my cheek,
Or was it a petal of a wayward flower?
I fell on my knees,
Embracing the hushed tamarack-pine tree.
You stared at me,
And day-dreamed a forest.

Inner Sense Of Touch

June 16, 2012

When my world shrinks,
I retreat
Within the hollow
Of my home.
I feel a presence
Confounding me
Ribbons of light,
A flash of yellow streaks
He kisses me
While I dream
Of patterns
Shocked with bent colors,
His shadow
Slips away,
But I am aware
Of his love.
He soothes my inner wounds.
I spin a potters' wheel
In my spare room.
Sending him a bright star-burst vase,
Created from my
Inner sense of touch.

Chaos

June 22, 2012

Quiet,
I place the iridescent
Gingham shawl
Around me.
I feel the gentle pressure
Folding over me.
I hear sudden shifts
In my soul-room,
The leather scent of books
Sought by the Seekers of Knowledge,
The subtle shade of parched pages,
Metaphorical shapes
Elude me.
I remember those sharp symbols
Before my mind
Spilled away from the material world;
An inner turbulence;
I lost balance and harmony.
The curved notes and their verbal musical sounds
Were cacophonous
I lost my focus.
Whirling, the dizziness
Shocked me
Rapid eye movements;
I cannot see!
Fluttering, the beat of my heart.
I fell into a mine of chaos.

Haiku, The Bengal Cat

June 28, 2012

My irises
Are slit
When I breathe in the luminescence
Of a reflected mirror.
In candlelight,
My almond-colored pupils are voluminous
Like the mysterious perspicacity
Of my Bengal cat, Haiku.
She purrs
And does not shun me,
Curled, spotted like a leopard;
She is often on my lap
Heavy and somnolent
Beside or on me,
Intuitively warming me,
And healing me
From the blood-color
Of stress.
She is a meditation;
My breathing becomes
Steady and penetrating
Deep and focused.
I do not need a mantra;
The continuous purr
Vibrates, massaging me
When I hyperventilate
From the demands of the day;

I am often broken
As I seek the wonder
Of the world of words,
Shadows escape me,
And I am awestruck.
Haiku is sylvan and wild
As we play together
In the ruins of a woodland
Swallowed by the daisies.

I Am A Wraith

June 30, 2012

I stained his lips,
With my blushing lip-balm.
My vision was expectant.
His fatigue,
Evolves from a psychic drain,
Sharing long, relevant hours
sapping his worldly energy.
I introduce a Nepalese singing bowl;
I encircle the hand-made
Metal bowl
With a wooden stick;
The bowl sings.
And creates tonal vibrations
To calm his spirit.
Flute and harp music
Surround the interior rim
Of my house.
I place sacred candles
Around his tub,
As his stress is diminished
Into the uncongealed fluids
Spilling over his body.
He easily enters his office,
Working feverishly;
His intensity, his addiction.
Often, he forgets
That I exist.
I feel rebuffed;

I am but a wraith,
who permeates the plentitude
Of my sanctuary.
My lover's French doors lock
Him into his alcove.
Creation is no illusion.
I try to beguile him
With my carefully
Selected perfume,
Anointed 'Romance.'
His work is holy;
His conceptions will heal the world
With the depth of his research
And shocking linear intentions.
I return to my Ashtamangal Singing Bowl,
Hand crafted in Nepal.
I fill my sanctuary with white lilies,
And dissolve into
My sun room
With green and rose-colored leaves,
Where my cat, Haiku, purrs on the day-bed.
My plants absorb
The long-singing tone
Of a holy metal bowl.
He seeks my love, punctually, late into the night.
I am renewed in the dawn
Where I seek the surface of the sun.

Descending Into Silence

July 4, 2012

I was shattered.
My inner struggle
Channeled me
Toward the dark aspect
Of the moon,
Or a solar eclipse,
The interior well
With black,
Heavy water;
Profusion;
My inner soul
Departed
Within my hidden effusion
Of pain
I was deaf;
Descending into silence.
Sheltered into my heart's center
I hollowed out a space,
Where I developed
A divergent language;
Only my outer body was visible.

My Thoughts Entwine My Very Being

June 21, 2012

The sun mocks me,
So I will day-dream,
Shaded
Under the leaf-spotted dew
Of a willow tree
I light a scented candle
Placed lovingly
On my round white table,
Drinking sparkling water.
The sky's tone is sepia
Even though I breathe
In a tempest
Of my sudden impressions;
My thoughts entwine my very being
Like ivy surrounding my brick and stucco home.
Leaves and centering trees with lush branches
Protect me from white-gold burning rays.
My skin is not parched or dehydrated.
I choose a soft shelter
As I am enclosed from a harsh
And piercing pain.

Origami Folds

July 16, 2012

Origami folds,
A paper crane,
In harmony to the textured sheets
Bound within my books
I cherish these hidden words;
They transcend
Beyond the limits
Of my present knowledge.
They, too, expose the trees
That gives them life.
A Japanese screen
Signifies images of light,
As it cuts
One room,
A private studio,
Slicing a spacious living room.
There are no walls.
Driven to create,
I embrace an art-form
With its own rhythm,
I sing-out the words
Like a living play,
Or a Japanese haiku.
Five-seven-five,
A singular art,
A form of meditation,
Centered within a poetic mantra.

Green-And-Spent Passion

July 24, 2012

I have emerged
Out of shapes
And hidden lacerations
That once pierced
My human-shell;
A humming-bird
Is quick
And illuminating.
I watch her
Presence from
My soothing crescent window
Reflecting the outside world of
Green-and-spent passion,
Survival and dissolution.
A woodpecker
Tends to the yearning tree,
Shallowly cutting
Through several layers of bark.
This bird's plight
Is mine
As I nourish
My own nature,
Evolving within
A precious and transient moment.

Enduring Love

July 31, 2012

I need an enduring love,
Constant,
I am unsteady,
My words are tangled
Like my unruly long hair.
When I awaken
From the dread of my dreams.
Diabolical wings
Reside in the center-of-my-being.
Memories torment me.
I wish to expunge
The torture of my child-world.
I need you
To dwell, every season,
Within my house,
And my fluttering heart.
I will not overwhelm you.
I seek stability.
I soar,
Though, often, I descend,
Intuitively, within the dominion
Of my heart, rupturing.
I, like a Geisha,
Can purify your past
Singing, in a soprano voice,
My intimate words.
I vow that I will shape my secrets
Through abstract phrases.

I am not linear.
Soothing herbs
And exotic spices are precious, as you are precious.
I share a cup of green tea with you, my love.
I am vigilant;
I, too, am your muse
And your spirit-guide
As I share my voluminous knowledge—seeking books
That mix words, rarely clouding my vision.
I am your tree of life,
My flowers flourish—a moon-burst.
You were stunned by my
Artistic-shelter,
Though the shadow of my images
Retreats into my sleep.
I often shift, twisting the sheets,
I am in flux.

My Secret Code

August 13, 2012

Sand-lily,
A spring herb.
Delicately sprinkled
On my egg-plant.
My subtle perfume
Blends into the
Pre-cooked sauce,
My cat, Haiku,
Licks the bowl
As if the fusion
Dispersed into catnip.
My concoction was savored
As the thicket
Brushed against
Our stone-bench
Where my love
Pressed a talisman
Into my hands.
The engraving blessed me,
'poetry is prayer.'
Though I am rarely resilient,
He sanctioned
My path.
And cultivated
My coping skills.
As we consecrated
With our chalice of Bordeaux
My secret code,
'Poetry is prayer.'

I Choose Bees-Wax

August 14, 2012

Candles
Made with ashes.
I choose bees-wax.
I don't exist at a time
That seizes curiosity,
Where women
Wore shapeless clothes
Hanging loosely
On their fragile frames.
Their hems swept
The dusted floor,
They choose shiny and deadly.
They were not fearful.
Lost were their masks
That repel germs
As they entered the nursery
Of a flu-ridden child;
They scrubbed floors
Like self-flagellation;
They could not bare their souls;
Imprisoned
They abused themselves
With guilt and mania.
While men
Spoke with acidity
Their damning words,
"Clean my house
Cook my meals."

The women
Could not reflect;
There was no inner life
Or self-awareness,
Their education?
Only a sick work-ethic,
They were always cleaning,
Stirring, shifting
Until their self-brutality
Stressed them into a stroke,
They died young.

Stained-Glass Reflections

August 18, 2012

A fractured family home,
Chaos, sewage, a metal bookcase,
Torn and worn chairs of foreboding.
No art, no treasure;
Few windows,
As I write in the darkened room,
Void of light,
Inlaid lead paint,
Colors intrude
The environment
Sordid, with the brown, grey and black crates.
Overall misery
Seeps through the rooms,
Junk,
Tables pressed over the cords
Threatening fire.
My disquietude,
An inevitable fusion
Of smoke and flames.
I seek a sanctuary,
A refuge from my insidious deprivation.
Or an illusion of safety.
Now, years later,
My obsession
Of blossoming, pliant bougainvilleas
Thrive without distress.
I am now blessed
With solace and light.

I have rose windows,
And stained-glass reflections,
Shaping an evolving sun,
Shimmering and radiant.
My refuge,
Of flowers, miniature pink roses,
Centered on my mahogany table and in my heart.
The oak-wood floors and doors,
I honor them
As I would a tree-filled forest.
Rugs and paintings are imbued
With patterns and radiance,
Patches of color
Enveloping each room,
Set apart with circumspection,
I create my own myths,
My perspective of beauty
As I unlock my special music-box
Where I dream of my present and unique reincarnation
While listening to Beethoven's Fifth Symphony.

The Arch Of The Sky

August 20, 2012

Infused flowers,
I elude my body,
Yet,
My spirit is tree-high
floating
As I regard myself,
Immobile
Within the verdant knoll
With a semblance of sleep;
Yet I grasp
My time has ceased.
For me to heed
The drops of dew,
Enveloping me like an aura,
Whispering through the trees' element.
I am into the firmament,
The arch of the sky.
Waves of a sudden tsunami
Released me.
My rapid heart-beat is now mute;
I no longer panic.
My unsettled pulse
Is quelled.
I follow the Tao,
The way is fleeting.
The clouds unfold,
A distinct universe
Engulfs me.

My mind is soothed and subtle;
No more intense mania
Or crippling melancholy;
Gravity is no longer leaden;
Bury my heart.
People say that I am still comely,
Before I enter the white coffin.
Now, I am remote
Within the Hall of Souls.

Pressed Like A Dried Lily

August 24, 2012

Bereft of light,
Displaced,
When I hid
In the closet,
I was enveloped
With excessive robes,
Devoid of her day-dresses
And their mutable colors;
A white light,
Glared through
The pinnacle of the sheaved door,
A mist of sweet perfume,
I gagged,
I cupped my hand,
Like an invisible sheath pressing
Into my vision.
My eyes were tearing.
Sharply, the breaking of dishes
And the shiver of a broken glass.
I cherished
Those dishes, the flourishing lush blossoms,
Hibiscus
And butterflies, a lovely ornamentation
Patterns painted the ivory background.
I resolved
Never to bond with another psyche,
The chapters
Of their past,

Their mendacity,
Disoriented me.
After an elapsed time.
Their scent of longing
Could ruin me.
Their shadows drained themselves,
Throughout the achromic,
Musty and infusion of mold;
Their uneven moods
Pressed, like a dried lily,
In their book of the night.

The Music Box

September 8, 2012

This key,
Opens my music box;
I listen to the light
And atmospheric timbre.
Evanescent,
The intricacy
Dissipates my distress,
Where obliterated memories
Swiftly emerge;
I am beyond enduring
The horror,
I was inarticulate
As if in collusion with my tormenters.
Malevolence;
My struggle for sanity.
I open the music box;
I have tripped my mindset,
I am a witness;
Of the memory, a Holocaust.
I open the music box
And am moonstruck
Where music sighs and dreams collide.
Beethoven's Fifth Symphony
Purging me, for a transient moment,
My unspoken secret,
That my life ceased years ago
As if strangled on my umbilicord

In this parallel universe
I believe in the essence of the music box.
My key opens and dilutes my madness.

An Ochre Horse

September 11, 2012

A visionary force
Penetrated my dream.
An ochre horse,
His placid demeanor
Nudging his essence
As I stroked him.
My dream morphed
Into a nightmare
Of turmoil and disquiet.
Most of my anterior consciousness
Was a refuge from chaos
Dance and music
Were secret codes
That kept me vivified.
I cultivated a
Raw existence,
Even though
I was pursued
Oh, by the anguish of my oblivion.
The horse,
This clear, pure essence,
my divine-seeker,
took flight as we circumvented a tempest.

This specter
Revealed his purpose psychically,
He resolved
To eradicate
My fathomless trauma;
So now,
I call forth
My sentient being,
Under the aegis of his soul.

Intrinsic Camouflage

September 12, 2012

A hurt creature settles in,
Like her lacerations.
This wee chipmunk
Enters the garden
The weeds are benign.
She chews
The cluster of cyclamen,
Her pain subsides;
A shard of a flower-bud
Succumbs, deepening the moist-soil.
Her energy is depleted.
She is weary of predators,
Her gait is slow
As if she was pregnant;
She is endangered,
She needs to run within the darkness,
Shade herself into
A nebulous grotto,
She perceives her intrinsic camouflage;
Her shattered soul has cut into her aura,
Now, she is no longer revealed.
She will not divulge her secret;
Or live a haunted life;
She will prevail.

Over The Rim Of Clouds

October 11, 2012

Pegasus
Lost sight
Over the rim of clouds.
His translucent wings shuddered.
He sought me like a melody
As I stroked the keyboard
While he was harkening
To the depth of my pain.
His intuition was raw.
His breath intermingled
With my gasp
Induced by the floating pollen.
I hollowed out
A mystic cave
For his ubiquity.
His flight was in harmony
With the treble clef
Of my own song's desire.
I would not desist.

Perceived Through A Lattice

October 18, 2012

The color of the gust of wind
Blends with the yellow and bronze trees.
Poison ivy is the deterrent
In their webbed leaves,
Until they are swept away.
When the sky dims,
The shadows shape and shift
Into an abstract ardor
That appears as a mirage.
My focus is bent,
Slanted like the rain
That nestles my window
Hushed by the northern wind.
In the mist
My view,
Perceived through a lattice,
Resists generative white stains.

A Wreath

October 23, 2012

A seraph,
Evolves into the mist.
She seeks the warmth
Of my fireplace and
Its luminosity
This specter
Is unaware of my discernment.
She writes her longing on parchment
Or sheepskin.
She reveals her poetry.
Her mind is distorted
And oblique.
She is perverse,
Her vision breaks all the rules
I place a wreath,
For her silver-white hair
On my mahogany table,
As a celebration
Of her spent and subtle words
And I slip away
Beyond fear.
Ink flows throughout my fingers.
In a burnt color.
Her loving aura
Resides in my heart,
And, like twins,
Our shadows intertwine.

Red Is Vibrant Or Violent

October 25, 2012

Gardenias
Spill over my grass-land.
My yard is surreal,
White apples sweeten the trees,
Colors change with the northern light,
I dream in shades of lime and blue;
Red is vibrant
Or violent;
My fear of blood.
Menstruation is nourishing.
Fecundity is worshipped.
Yet look at the saints?
I remained virginal,
With an aloofness
Toward men and danger.
Puberty was perilous
Where I could be thrust
Within the horror
Of the desolate, dark city,
I only knew strife
As I was perishing
And struggling for the renewal
Of the hushed doom of morning,
Even though I lived under a stained-glass dome,
Shedding and releasing the colors of my night-side.
I, safely, ran away, with the flying dust.
I lived in a one-room claustrophobic apartment
When I was almost assaulted and raped

Where I succumbed to the wisdom
Of multiple locks
That shielded my heart's song.
Pine-trees germinated in the isthmus
Of a near park.
I sought stark benches
Where I prayed.
My blood would leak,
Staining my softly blown sepia-colored skirt,
Recalling my terror
Of pregnancy and loss.
I would release my child
To a barren couple.
Or I would perish
Or miscarry
This sacred being.
Homelessness was not an option.

The Mystery Of My Body

October 26, 2012

My shapeless mud-stained dress,
No hint of flow,
Erasing the curve of my delicate ankle,
Or the wind defining the mystery
Of the essence of my body.
Now, I choose that hint of subtle sensuality,
The soft breast,
Elongated earrings
Framing my face;
Though, often,
My hair sweeps down
Like a hood;
My features are blurred
As I hide myself from temptation.
The clothes define me;
Barefoot, I lean against
The cherry trees
Experiencing their earth tones
In harmony
With my season's colors.
My black velvet open-toed shoes
Now, displaced beside me,
Are in tune with the soft, sweet
Crumbling loam,
Beware of the peat bog.
The sensory gardens
caress the textured, oval leaves

as my hand senses my obscured vision.
All my other senses are lucid.
I have crystals in my inner ear
Which like an abrasion
Defines me with a slight vertigo.
I awaken while meditating
To the spinning birch-trees and the
Asymmetrical wooded thicket, shrubs and hedges
While the sand piper and meadowlark
Tremble in their songs, a pastoral.
I can sing the tones of a flute from a waters reed,
Or a mandolin
With my dulcet voice
Resonating beside the gentle timbre
Of a shimmering waterfall.

The Tenant Of My Heart

October 30, 2012

Once again
You are away,
Even though
You will always be
The tenant
Of my heart.
I am wasted,
So I sustain
All the greenness
Of my plants
As they reside
Within the summer of my house
Where the southern light bleaches
My oak-wood floors,
And where my spotted, Bengal cat
Breathes in the earth's bounty.
I can descry
My own heart beating
While I arise to this solitude.
My books
Console me.
The soul within the book
Is released,
Like an incorporeal being,
Enriched with wisdom
And never suppressed,
Yet, anticipating my presence.
The sea-filled air

Is salt and wonder.
I have an abundance
Of this placid silence,
A barrier
To the exterior sharpness of the spectral wind.
I have succumbed to the tenderness of your smile.

The Pearl Bracelet

November 2, 2012

I wear
The pearl bracelet
That you bestowed
On my wrist.
The pearls are luminous;
They share the ocean
Like you are the distilled water,
And I am the reservoir
That erupts from the rocks,
Or shapes into its marrow of stillness.
The fish should not be injured,
Even if they are crustaceans.
I vowed to sustain myself
On vegetables;
But my iron is diminished.
Like the Jainists,
I try to overlook
The horror
Of abattoirs,
Where animals,
Are cruelly treated.
I cherish all sentient beings,
I protect my cat from anguish
Or illness;
She is compliant.
Animals, often, live in despair,
They are spiritual
And yet they vanish,

Thrust against
Their reliance on water,
The loam, the humus
And the clay.
Who are the predators
With obscured empathy?

Their Frail Embrace

November 5, 2012

My face is pale,
Then flushed
As water cascades
Down my hair
Now stringy
With tear drops and rain.
My eyes fill with condensation,
As my reminiscence
Engulfs me unevenly.
I am loosely unadorned
My shawl is amorphous.
Bright colors descend
Fading within this grey mist.
Wandering yellow-white leaves
perish on my distinct wind-blown skirt
Where silk-worms entwined
My delicate, complex threads.
The tree trunks are unguarded,
Their frail embrace
Has lost their bounty
As I am brittle.
Their limbs await an ice-storm
Which seals their aspect.
They have shed their vibrant blooms.

With My Heartbeat

November 9, 2012

The pendulum of
My grandfather clock
Beats in rhythm
With my heartbeat.
It is the passion of my house
Speaking with true eloquence,
Whispering to my psyche
And my instincts.
My fireplace
Is the vision of my house,
Its brilliant glow is somnolent,
I bury my fluid cognition.
My massive, arched window
Reflects the zenith of vulnerable trees,
As nature's kinetic energy,
Mingles with the purity of my spirit.
My books and music
Illuminate me, as I perceive
The opening passage of my emotions
Into the depth, like lime-water,
Of my very being.

I Was Never Praised

November 10, 2012

I was never praised
When I was a child,
I was never praised
When I was a poet and musician,
I was never praised when I was ballet dancer
My husband criticizes me all the time.
I was never praised
By white males
Who rule
The academic world.
Everywhere I am struggling
Not to fail,
As I constantly fail.

Understanding Men

November 11, 2012

My throat contracts,
A sad possibility that I cannot share
My inner nest
Where I belong.
Attempting communication
Without blame.
Perhaps I can find
His hidden depth,
Without hurting him
With my slight moodiness,
And defensiveness.
I can complete his sentences
Even though I am raw.
When he rages against his past.
I will guide him.
I will not withdraw.
His explosive metaphors are necessary
For his nuclear release.
I am in pain
As I watch him struggle
With the complexity of his
Attempt to commune with me.

Core Fears

November 12, 2012

Our love
Cannot be tainted.
We share both the sun and the moon,
Sometimes the tide
Bursts from its frozen state
And is mutable,
It shifts the sand
And scars our emotions.
You were not cherished
When you were tender,
And vulnerable.
You now shift your awareness
Throughout their malignancy
Your father bludgeoned you;
However, you sought your survival.
You fought against his shame.
I was a castaway,
Yet I blossomed
Into the artist
And the healer
I will protect you
From your core fears.

Vital Fluid

November 12, 2012

You are my pulse,
I need a tourniquet
As my blood would spill
From my fingers
Like ink,
Where I would write
My book's heart,
The deckle-edged parchment
Is not stale.
It is framed
Against the back drop
Of my Alpaca throw
Hung against my wall
Aside my macramé
That I created
For my bewitchment
Toward you.
The lariat,
Did not reach my heart
Like my written words;
Though I bled life into
Its essence.
A creation is an elixir
Like a black cat
Revealing herself;
Like an amulet,
Imbued with charm, hope and love;
I am a shamanist.
Where I share my remedy
With my life's vital fluid.

The Aperture Of My House

November 14, 2012

I sliver carrots
Like coleslaw,
My garden
Is bordered by the copse.
The plenty of tomatoes and watermelon,
But mainly bougainvillea
And dahlias,
A diminutive apple tree.
I respire their scent
And am placed in a trance
By their burnished sheen,
Where a small stone pathway,
Leads to our Adirondack chairs
Of lime and blue,
Colors, alive
Like sea-birds,
Mythical birds;
Cast as a rainbow.
My basket links
With my arm,
As I wander
With delicacy,
Within the aperture of my visionary house,
With its own perfume
Of rosewater, lavender and musk.

The Sea, The Mist, The Fells

November 27, 2012

Darkness,
As I slip over my fear
Of cliffs and the illuminated
Green and haunted fells,
Many clouds burst
While the sun is unguarded
There are signals of rain,
A conscious rhythm.
I am cloistered in
Wordsworth's Dove Cottage
In Grasmere,
In The Lake District
Of England.
Later, I am drenched with mist
And visions,
Striking hallucinations
Emanate in my octagon room.
I dream of Coleridge
Whose room is organic.
His scent is desolation.
And opium,
His elixir extending his life.
Shelley bonded with Wordsworth's terrestrial sphere.
I, also, would bond with Shelley.
As I seek out a kindred country
The sea, the mist, the fells,
The voices of the dead
stranded beneath the sod.
Would seclusion ruin my ingenuity,
Or nurture me with the lure of the cosmos?

Whispering

December 3, 2012

Whispering,
The night wind,
I await the splash of sunshine,
In the dawn.
All evening,
I searched for sound,
Is it a humming-bird?
The voice bleeds
Implicit words.
I search the sun room;
So many crescent plants,
Subtle curved arms of seedlings
Now overgrown and resplendent,
The untilled substance
Releases blithely
In their southern exposure
Nourishing and untainted;
My tall, stained-glass lamp,
Pure luminosity.
Infused with color.
I remember
Turning off this light.
What is that humming
I descry?
I will take a token,
your feather
Little bird,
You are my mystic.

Engraved On The Essence Of My Soul

December 7, 2012

The lucency
Of a candle,
An Attar of roses;
I contemplate
And pray to my mother's
Departed spiritual psyche,
The flame is evocative of her memory,
She did not deserve
To be insolvent,
The desolate environment
Rejecting her artistry,
Her drawings
Her love of music
And dance and literature.
My father was soulless,
He shunned
Creative imagination
As I interpreted an adagio
And a polonaise.
While expressing poetry,
I danced the pirouette.
Music was engraved
On the essence of my soul.
I, now, can strike the highest note,
The complex chords;
Legato is fluid and healing.
The sharps and the flats
No longer challenge me;

My heart beats deeply,
Placating my distress
In tune with my music.
I dream of Bach and Chopin.
My nourishment was withheld.
The candle's flame
Releases my mother's loss.
The perfume's nectar
Fills the void.
It is placed, gently, on top of my piano.
Now, my mother is painting on her palette
With an ardent Spirit
Perfecting her destiny.

Angel Eyes

December 9, 2012

In the midst of my mortality
I am sanctified
In my shelter,
Where I share fragile treasures
And hope.
My lover is on a journey,
A land into the wind
Seeking wisdom.
I am placated,
And summoned
By a white rose,
Albino,
As I replenish my blessings.
Playing the subtle music
Of a French folk-song.
I blend the white rose
Within a Juniper wreath,
It scatters throughout
The pine cones
And holly,
As I discern the rose,
the Angel eyes.

A Gift

December 9, 2012

An Alberta Spruce Tree,
Copious,
Bordering my window,
As you are benevolent
And uniquely precious
And tender,
As you bestow
Me with bountiful gifts
Of gold lace
And candles.
You are chivalrous,
A fragment of antiquity
That had been obscured
Or hidden,
You are enigmatic
And, often, reticent,
Still, you are stunned
By my phrases,
As I spill and cling to my words
After embracing you.
I bestow you with a melody.

Bewitched

December 13, 2012

I want to be sublime
And untainted,
Not impaired.
By human foibles.
Am I unattainable
When I speak to my muse
While in solitude?
Within my environs
I am so focused
Within my astral body;
I rarely hear
The ringing of my phone,
I read,
In my blue chaise lounge,
Oblique phrases;
I share my mind's space for you,
But not the window of my deviation.
The star grass
Is planted
Water-deep long days.
I partake of Belladonna,
My pupils wide-eyed and astonished.
I am bewitched.

An Inlet

December 14, 2012

The world is so big
And I am
Just a breath
In the nebula of Orion;
I recover stars,
That are lost
In the quickening
Of my pulse;
Am I alone?
I reach out to you,
With star-dust,
We flux
Into our own nature.
Avoiding the ravaging
Ozone layer
Sun-blots
And radiation.
We drive away
The storm-showers
As we hide in an inlet,
Sheltered from
The moon-crash.

My Spirit

December 19, 2012

My spirit
Is released;
It is extraneous,
It floats
Around you, my love.
Even as I sleep,
Dreaming horrific memories;
A childhood's past is never gone.
It sneaks
Into your unconscious,
And suddenly,
You are deluged with grief.
I will do everything to make
You happy.
And when
The sand-storm
Reduces my vision,
I reach out
And I protect you.

My Nectar

December 19, 2012

Cull the crops,
Germinate the sprouts,
Chards, turnips, kohlrabies.
The fragrant loam,
The clay
Nurturing,
Organic vegetables,
Like I nourish you
With my magnum opus,
Brahms "Lullaby"
and Bach's "Well-Tempered Clavier,"
I speak to you
In communion,
I write to you with my nectar,
My secret codes
That are blessed in cerulean ink.
I am your Venus
And your Aphrodite.

My Hearth

The phosphorescence
Within my hearth,
Reflects
The heat
That never withers.
My heart filled moods
Burning in motion,
My valves are rhythmic,
Beating in unison
With your essence.
Replenishing
The depth of my silence.
We face each other's
Opaque eyes;
Entwined,
Our lips touch,
And timidly
Your arms enfold my breasts,
As you follow the thread
Of my tawny hair,
Now wrapped around
My pale cheeks,
And cerise lips,
My delicate
And slender fingers
And untinted tapering nails
Glide along the façade,
The vellum of your skin.

The tempest
Intrigues the woods,
The raw bark,
The sharp ice
Is outside our solemn shelter,
A retreat
With the hearthstone's glow.

His Element Is Silver And Iridescence

January 16, 2013
For my loving husband, Richard

I succumbed to his love
As I focused on my path.
I could only give him my muse,
And my music
As well as my redemption,
His gifts were beyond
My own alloy,
His element
Is silver and an iridescence
Like cultured pearls.
We built our house
Of light and wood.
I was alluring
Sharing my silken threads
With his bed of red buds;
He merits
All my musing,
My interior string of words,
Fleshed out
To nurture him.
On a whim
He bestowed me with
My canto
And oak-wood bookcases.
He cherishes my scrolls.
My keyboard sings
Along with a metronome.

His choice of light,
A rainbow,
Flourishing throughout
My sanctuary.
He expanded the bright rays.
My window glistens.

Psychic Wounds

January 28, 2013

Whispering and quietude
Are displaced.
The cold season
Shuns rays of sounds
The tonality
Of feelings dilate,
Yet they are not discernable.
You fear the depths,
Fluctuations and spontaneity
Of emotions.
You recall the terror of rages
That diminished your childhood
And your resources.
The expressive arts,
And musical notes
Were scorned.
Your interests were nullified
I lured you
With my trills
And rhapsodies.
My fugues and etudes,
My early years of pirouettes
That graced me
Into a theta state.
These meditations
Bound my psychic wounds.

Our Coupling

February 6, 2013

Lorn,
I lament
Your crossing of the seas,
Seeking cloud-swept mountains;
You are the guru
Of precious unrestrained wisdom,
I am a broken shell
Pieced together
When you rebound,
As I am no longer a recluse.
A fragment of my essence
Yearns toward my
Need to be multifaceted,
As I strive to impress
My solemn and subtle intuitions
Toward our coupling.
You are an astral being
As you release the shock of the sun.

Warm As Fleece

February 11, 2013

A dovetailed basket
stitched in links
Like a complex spider's web
Or a Jacquard weaver.
The bounty
Of provolone, lambrusca grapes,
And pinot noir
Reward us with our bounty.
Our arms entwine,
So I, supplicant, partake of your feast
And you drink my viscid nature;
The zealous wind
Unfurls my surrounding light grey ruana.
Its Moorish design is singular.
The sandalwood and myrrh incense
Soothes away nullifying thoughts;
We are entranced with each other,
Tears of elation
Waters the soil,
Even though the slight snow
Impedes the fullness of this bobolink's feathers.
Its coat is warm as fleece.

The Summer Of Stones

February 22, 2013

Sweet butter,
Thai vegetables
Remind me
Of felicity
The summer of stones,
Trailing along the Buddhist parkway,
A garden of solidity
This temple embraces me
As I view the purified altar,
A liturgy of karma.
I also postulate in the euphoric
Bursting lotus blossom
Replicating the light of the One
Who guides me out of my affliction
With the wonder of
The seraphic essence of healing herbs,
A tonic
Dissolving my corporeal pain.

The Secret

February 25, 2013

The secrets
Held deeply inside me;
The ruins of my memory.
The roof is displaced
The lithic stone is exalted.
I seek feather-pens
Dipping the ink on rice paper
And illuminating my manuscript.
The Orient
Haunts me.
I dismiss the warrior cult,
And I melt
Into the cities of Kyoto
And Nara.
I am reverent;
I bow my head
And speak in tongues
My inception
Was the distant secret
Of my fate.
I heard voices
Enlightening me
Of our bond
I am the mistress of
Our Asian domain.
I am one with the house.

Mythical Flowers

February 27, 2013
We cannot sow seeds with clenched fists.
To sow we must open our hands.
—Aldolfo Perez Esquivel,
Argentine architect, sculptor, human rights leader,
1980 winner of the Nobel Peace Prize

My lineage
Gathered dust
And sudden symptoms of rage
She purged her wondrous mind,
Now stolen by
Scarred walls,
Windows swallowed
By streaks of squalid mud;
A catatonic silence,
Or fulminating
A convulsion
Of a grim visage.
I was always thirsty,
My tongue was
Swollen by salt-water.
The air was tainted;
The grey colors were faded,
Her angst
Pressing down on her
Like a heated iron.
Laundry spilled over
The shredded carpet;
Her arms and legs permeated

Rivulets of blood
Freeing her
From the anguish of her psyche.
After I entered the seasons
And rhythm of your shattered heart.
We were intertwined.
I was besotted
By your tender nature,
I was blessed with empathy
And evaded havoc.
We propagated the winter flowers.
They were mythical.

Afterlife

March 1, 2013

The sky seems swollen-grey
Against the sun
Like a moody squall.
My melancholy
Pours inward
Like the afterlife.
I need pastels,
A flourish
Of bright colors,
Wild rose and light
There is no bird in sight.
The hushed tones are wistful;
My eyes sweep the trees
Barren, untilled,
Farewell my season's leaves.
I beckon a wild bird;
I may as well be mute;
He will not rejoin;
Even the wind is not aroused.
I pace from room to room
Looking for some object that sparkles.
Seeking my teapot,
And two delicate vessels linked
With cream and sugar,
Silver-plated,
I pour myself Jasmine tea.

The Arms Of Morpheus I

March 4, 2013

Enigmatic sleep,
I am frozen in opaque dreams.
There is no where to hide
As I am assaulted
Within the arms of Morpheus.
I panic,
As if I was abducted
And devoured by the incubus.
My alarm clock
Is my only hope.
The vestiges of sleep
Brand my shattered day.
My memories are toxic;
I am in a state of stupor
Until the softening pace of dusk;
I pray for wisdom
As the red bare sun,
Befalls the horizon.

The Lady Of White Flowers

March 5, 2013

Our souls are combined,
A ghost
Of a Lady of White Flowers
With the scent of lavender
Floats with the turbulence,
Of waves that palpitate
And seek the pulsating
Blood of my mystic heart.
My vicarious emotions
Predispose me toward
The fragrant water-flowers.
I dispose of the deluge
That leaks through the window-panes
As cracks drip through my ceiling.
The vestige
In my music room.
The flow and design of clear water
Is subtle.
It never pours on my piano.
The Lady of White Flowers
Comforts me.
She is the mistress of my tears;
I weep profusely,
And I will be embraced.

The Threaded Grass

March 8, 2013

The wind
Wastes away
The threaded grass
surrounding my stone bench.
They cling to each other,
Struggling to survive
They curl with each breath.
The weather
Hints at the filament's demise.
I intend, falsely, to cope with loss;
The fragility of life
The disconnection
Of raw dreams,
Shaping my own mortality.
I cannot live without you—
My stellar patron
Of my muse.

My Talisman

March 08, 2013

Tibetan prayer beads
Surround my wrist.
It repels the malevolence
Of the evil eye.
Within my own conception,
I am camouflaged,
Almost invisible.
Only wood creatures
Envelope me,
They are inculpable.
A squirrel
Shares her food,
An acorn nut,
Which she deposits
On my bare arch,
My talisman, the bracelet, the beads,
Bless her.
Her predators
Will overlook her.
My outdoor tasks
Include a small maze
Of durum and bushes;
There is no need for a fence.

Starlight

March 09, 2013

The Little Dipper,
Pleiades,
Ursa Major,
Astound me
I dwell at the edge of the slight foam.
Of a tranquil estuary.
The hallowed light
Reflects the rainwater,
Streaming over me.
A stirring
In my day dreams;
I realize that there
Are no clouds.
The milky way
Is dominant.
I feel infinitesimal.

The Windows Are Invulnerable

March 11, 2013

Liquid sunshine,
A tendril untwines,
The vapor
Drips on my fine, brown hair,
An ivory and beaded barrette,
Blushes red
With subtle tints.
A full thread of my tresses
Is clasped
Near the nape of my neck.
The dampness
Surrounds the soil.
The silt
Reveals the subsistence
Of chipmunks
Meadowlarks and loons.
The worms are revealed.
My native home
Its windows are invulnerable.
But I am walking at the border
Of an aviary and lush thickets,
As I am restored
By the soft song-drops
Of the rain.

Song-Drops Of The Rain

March 11, 2013

Liquid sunshine,
A tendril untwines,
The vapor
Drips on my fine, brown hair,
An ivory and beaded barrette,
Blushes red
with subtle tints.
A full thread of my tresses
Is clasped
Near the nape of my neck.
The dampness
Surrounds the soil.
The silt
Reveals the subsistence
Of chipmunks
Meadowlarks and loons.
The worms are revealed.
My native home
Its windows are invulnerable.
But I am walking at the border
Of an aviary and lush thickets,
As I am restored
By the soft song-drops
Of the rain.

My Fragility Is Not A Curse

March 16, 2013

"I am enough"
My yoga nidra teacher
While swooning in the theta state.
This is my intention,
"You are enough."
My interior realm,
A sphere;
I am blessed;
I enshrined my poem
Dedicated to you.
The frame is consigned to your desk.
My empathy is not a deterrent.
My piano sings;
Your genius is sanctioned,
I am in awe.
Your multitude of journeys,
Floats through the dusted clouds
Perceiving the earth and the cosmos.
My focus is not submerged,
As I teach, I read, I write, and I play
Chopin's 'Nocturne'
And, often, Beethoven's 'Ode to Joy.'
Though you are sometimes critical,
You relax as I grasp your dreams.
I dwell in my sanctuary.
My fragility is not a curse;
My inner world is not frozen,
It bleeds with my source of life.

A Feather

March 19, 2013

I swallow my words
When you are distressed.
After you reach a state of calm,
I help you meditate;
I massage you.
Here, my love!
I bow to your spiritual energy.
I brew a boiling russet tea,
And pour it within your favorite vessel.
I am attuned to you,
Our bond brushes
Your being
With a feather.
The feather is a light green,
It gently soothes you
Your body is supple
Yet taut.
A gentle reminder of our being.
Green is both nurture and nature.
The color beholds grass.
It is separating
And repairing
The days of instant snow.
There are still puddles
Like a bird-bath.
A feather plummets from
The azure fathomless sky.

The Journal Of My Night

March 19, 2013
Without our memories, we would be lost to ourselves,
amnesiacs flailing around in a constant, unrelenting present.
—Charles Fernyhough, PhD, *Pieces of Light*

My past is evocative
A painful blur;
Each night,
I discern
A slanted dream,
A surreal fragment,
A phrase of memory,
A glint of sparks
That are aromatic
From the sudden heat.
I awaken
To an evanescent string
Of photographs,
A discursive interlude,
A seizure
Like a momentary epileptic shock;
I transcribe these moments
In the Journal of my Night.

Shadows In The Attic

March 22, 2013

Shadows in the attic;
A treasure chest.
A symbol of Venus lingered
As a porcelain doll,
Attired with a wedding dress,
Sheer silk
And a gossamer veil.
I have two connected rings,
Two silver hearts,
Inlaid with our birthstones
Garnet and opal.
I am daunted by
The placid and gentle doll,
I was never a bride.
When I met you
I was in a haze;
I reclaimed my essence
Of life
Your wisdom spoke to me.
We embraced
Vulnerable, entangled
My words spilled
Into fragments
Of magic realism.
Your clear and linear mind
Was my challenge.
You called my insights complex.

I vowed to emote
All my sunshine and secret shadows.
The doll the attic,
Is a token
Which permeates
Our coupling.
Our love is enshrined.
I summon the doll,
Her ivory dress is purified.
A veil covers my dark hair.

Homelessness

March 26, 2013

I was desolate
And destitute,
I would have perished.
My sanity was fragile,
My kinetic energy
Was depleted,
I had melancholia,
My autonomy
Was an illusion.
Where could I live?
Squalor and grime,
Dust-motes settled inside a courtyard door.
I curled within the threshold of a house of Zeus,
Or a demigod.
My body,
Stressed and frail,
Wounded, almost into oblivion.
By the travail
And exploitation of my childhood,
My inability to cope,
My handicap.
I never wanted to take the vow,
Due to my trauma,
My memories—I am an archivist
Fraught with internal scars.
Though I was in love;
I cherished him
And our submerged aspect of our demons.

I wanted to sustain myself;
My survival, a dead end,
I, in need of sustenance,
Skirting the border
Of my spirit.
My fractured body and the ache
Of my soul are coupled.
I was dependent,
And his protégé,
He loved me,
I am sequestered.
I, now, work with the indigent
And the imprisoned.
My allotment is modest,
My alliterative verse
Is treasured,
On my sonorous piano,
I play esthetic music
For his senses.
Our days are eloquent.

Cosmic Force

March 27, 2013

The sun bleeds,
The rays flood the storm.
Lunar flight
We reframe our memories,
So that they are bearable;
I will pray by drumming;
Native American wisdom;
The earth is existent;
Sand-painting,
Green rivers of
The terrestrial colors.
The glistening glass
Unbroken pieces of ice.
Emanating,
As we stream
The green Gaea,
Into a collage reflecting our cosmic force.

A Diadem

March 28, 2013

Warm evenings;
A picnic.
Greek yogurt
Pita bread with hummus,
Lush strawberries;
Perrier,
Green and white blanket.
Stolen hours;
The pleasure of torridness
Pegasus is visible,
This sky burns with stars
I am a scripter,
Writing of flight,
Abundance,
The velocity of white heat,
The mystery of the palatial diadem,
Reflecting our spherical terrene.

Clairvoyance

March 29, 2013

I am clairvoyant
I dream
Of the three goddesses of the Fates
Who determine the course of human life
A fresco on my wall,
I applied the pigment.
I, also, consigned a copy of the emblem
"The Praying Hands"
By Albrecht Durer
That graced my fireplace mantel;
An invocation.
My own image—my painting,
Was indicative of your face;
After I glazed your acrylic surface
The following day,
As I reflected,
You wandered beside me,
As I chose the cobblestone path,
A bewitching trail of green and red blossoms
Guiding us
At the Botanic Gardens;
To live is
To survive by treading water.
It rained.
Pools
And waterfalls.
An apparition at the rose garden
And Japanese gardens,

The sensory gardens
For the sun-blind,
And acres of prairie land.
You were adjacent to me.
I was silent.
The carillon bells
Sung in harmony;
At that moment
You spoke to me.
It was a verbal embrace.
We shared tea and croissants
At their cafeteria.
You were struck with awe
When you returned
To my small country house.
My painting was vivid.
An embodiment of your nature.

I Sketch Your Emotions

March 29, 2013

Thatched roof,
Pebbledash,
The dormer windows,
Plasterboard
One precious room
A hearthstone,
A silent flame
A scroll of calligraphy,
Of a haiku poem
Traced upon the rice paper.
I perform the tea-ceremony,
Your china-cup is stained
Yet pure, the color of rouge.
Politely, I bow
As you receive my single red posy.
The ash tree perceives my bay window.
I seek inspiration
You are my visitant
You dwell
In the room
Of my reflection
As I sketch
Your emotions.

The Narrow House

April 10, 2013

Shale
At this burial site,
The narrow house
Her coffin,
Deeply held into the
Loam,
The terrain
Is flowerless.
I place a bouquet
Of peonies
On her craggy home.
She was six when she
Fled this earth;
Unknown child;
You are no longer desolate;
You no longer need to resist
Your father
Like fury,
He broke your fragile neck.
His eruption,
Your fracture;
There but for the
Grace of God, go I.

Volcanos

April 15, 2013

Kilauea, Vesuvius
She perceives their indigo rim,
The black lava,
The Igneous rock;
Corrosion
Seeking a human child,
A virgin,
Swallowed,
Risking the embers
And vestiges of bone and flesh;
Her soul is evolved,
It cannot be consumed,
She is a phoenix.
She ascends
Shining her evening colors in the solar spectrum.
A glow like a mist,
The torrent purifies
Both the cirrus and cumulus clouds,
As she succumbs to her psychic dreams,
Awakening within the Elysian fields.

Stained Glass Butterflies

April 16, 2013

Butterflies
Stain-glass light
On my window.
Falcate Orange tip
They grace the sun.
They flash
Within my flight of memory.
When I met you,
I was begging to fly,
My thoughts could not
String words along the outer rim,
My loss of autonomy
Broke my hue, my wing;
Our home
Was my chrysalis,
My wings, like ice,
Broke into shards, disconnected.
As I was surrounded by a chrysalis,
Where was my affinity?
My refuge?
You were my patron;
My poetry rebounded,
My prose
Enveloped my sheathe
And my protoplasm;
Now, I am a butterfly.

A Hummingbird

April 16, 2013

I am brittle,
I easily crack,
Yet, I am like a pierced yet unopened egg,
My yolk is fluid.
Yellow stains me
Like the bleeding vessels
Which follow the throb of my heart.
You made my nest,
Now, I am a hummingbird,
You are my place of origin,
I am lyrical,
I hum in verse,
You welcome my songs,
Here, behold my fallen feathers,
Now, a laurel wreath, a garland
As I shed the residue of my vulnerability.
I am under the aegis of your love.

Persephone

April 18, 2013

The shadow of rain is grey,
Footsteps in the murky quick sand.
As I descend,
I grasp a branch,
Or a wayward root
Lighting bends
Toward the summit,
The wind-break
Of the Juniper tree,
Dusted
Like a sand storm
In a desert;
Sleeping flowers
Do not shed their buds,
They surprise the god of the wind
Or Hera, the Greek goddess.
Ceres misses her daughter,
Persephone,
Who brings forth
The abundance of the earth.
In the guise of Spring.
When winter swells with blue from cold.
She is confined,
By her vow to Hades,
The god of the underworld,
As I struggle from mud-formed puddles,
I perceive the awakening of a tulip.

Shared Waters

April 23, 2013
... that it is necessary to have five hundred a year
and room with a lock on the door if you are
to write fiction or poetry.
—Virginia Woolf, *A Room of One's Own*

My flight
Is stirring
The wind.
I am like Pegasus
I slip through mountains
Or fells.
You are my equestrian,
I carry you away
On the everlasting vapor
Of my scent.
My mortar and pestle
Releases the perfume
Of White Angelica,
A sacred oil
Ground from the tears
And petals of fleurs.
We drink from the same
Waters-of-sweet-seasons;
You gave me flight,
My emotions evolve
As we embrace.

Woodbine

April 25, 2013

I stopped at my copse of trees,
The dry
Five leaf woodbine,
A doe-eyed fawn
Was encircled
By my fence,
However,
She was unencumbered.
Earlier, she bound over my fence
Into my loosely strung firmament.
I hid her from predators,
She found this circle of my wood-light-hedge
As she was camouflaged
By the vestiges of my wild-ring-of-grass,
I refused to tame my small acre.
Our golden-colored-pattern
Shined with grains of wheat.

Circle Of Trust

April 28, 2013

My silver wedding ring
Sparkles of gems
The stones of our intention
A circlet of your vow of my eternal breath,
It will endure.
I will shed my shadow,
As I awaken to my rebirth
Throughout the cosmos.
We will pursue our secret galaxy,
This symbol,
A hieroglyph
For a future sylvan flush of top-soil—
An entry of green mist and grassland and maize
Of my circle of trust.

My Meadow

May 1, 2013

My meadow,
A pasture,
The fertile heath grass
And cattail,
The green sward is
The only cultivated field.
My small fairy-cottage
Of a hupertufa material
Is accented by a red wood door;
My stone bench
Attracts a snowshoe hare
Who leans toward the foot's bench
Resembling a dewclaw.
The two Adirondack chairs,
Are recycled in primary shades
Of green and blue.
The Thrush is on the bright-lit seat.
She chooses a healing green, like her nature, my nature.
I sit at my patio,
With a wrought iron candle holder.
The scent is cleansing and sweet,

A Love Potion

May 6, 2013

A candle
Scented with pineapple cilantro
And a bouquet of tulips
Symbols of my courtship.
I focused on the sweet-spicy redolence,
The flame enveloped the wick
The vapor
Whispered as a love potion;
Surrendering light-spells and amulets.
I befriended the birds,
The geese, the ducks
Feeding soft-cut-sourdough bread
My grass bench
Entwined and clinging
Onto this gazebo
In a woodland,
My vision of you,
Your obsession with me.
Your aura of a light green,
The shade of this Yankee candle
Encased in glass orb,
Our fingers touched while in this field of daisies,
Like twins,
Separation was not an option.

Goddess Of Abundance

May 8, 2013

My silver fountain pen,
Deckle-edged paper;
I write down
Hindu mythology,
Pensive words,
Include blessings,
And visual memory
While I attempt
To block the terrors
Of my sleep-induced shadows
I silently.
Even out the disquiet,
Shades of uneven grey;
Expressions on my cherry escritoire,
As they are released,
While I am cloistered in my sacred room,
Dreaming shapes of goddesses,
Lakshmi, blessed with abundance
Of creativity and insight.
I incorporate that mantra,
My cells vibrate.

Stone-Angels

May 9, 2013

The potency of music
The organ, devotion at Notre Dame
In Paris,
The Dorsey Museum—
Behold the Expressionists,
Rodin and Monet
The cemetery,
Stone-angels at Montparnasse
Silent and divine,
I hear them—the western wind,
Mist is released; the flowers rush up toward my being.
The grave sites
Of Simone de Beauvoir
Sleeping intertwined with John Paul Sartre,
A sacrament.
Baudelaire's poem,
"Fleur de Mal"
Embossed by Rodin.
My reverence of Sacre Coeur
A unicorn tapestry, now, graces our home.
A church, the language of contour, configuration and design.
Born of light.
My aorta beats
The blood of my
Own rhythm,
As my heart beats
And I bleed
With my own cuneiform

Poetry, music, and a charcoal sketch of my divine abode.
I muse upon my stained-glass window.
Imagery explodes throughout my prose;
Reaching toward the realm of
The sweet taste of honey.
I am given to reverie.

A Wooden Red Door

May 10, 2013

I piqued your interest;
I enchanted you
Because I had a stone fairy house
With a wooden red door.
I was fey.
Your language was linear;
An indigo bird
Would land in my world of circular flowers.
Only in a magic land
Would such wings
Possess me.
He is vibrant
And sings a fable;
He draws you
Toward my winding flagstone walk.
I arise.

Holy Rain

May 15, 2013

My vocation
Is to grow
Into a shadowless
Tree,
With pear-shaped leaves,
And light roots.
A saboteur
Rips away at my tenuous
And shimmering bark;
My footway,
Leads to the glimmering
Rose French window.
I cannot enter within its protective
Court-like space.
After dawn,
I am softly ruined,
I shed my birth,
Yet the cobwebs,
Like tiny filigree,
Surrounds me;
I am wet with holy rain.
I am not lost.
The following day
Of white-sun,
My seeds—rebirth.

Sunken Energy

May 18, 2013

Herbaceous plants,
Edible root,
Dried sage and oregano.
Lucerne
In a large steamer,
Havarti on the butterfly plate.
Often,
My energy is sunken;
I cannot finish your simmering,
Nourishing meal.
My life-force is weary.
Agitated sensitivity
While I imbibe caffeine.
I stumble,
I fall
Into the creases of my loveseat.
I ponder and brood.
Time after time
I struggle
Beyond my abilities;
I pursue my sun-faceted energy.
I open the light of my house,
The casement windows,
Like bleached white sheets,
The aura, the luster
As I shine,
While I succumb

To the scent of a bayberry candle;
Though wan,
With a strenuous flow,
I return toward the gas stove.

The Ash

May 18, 2013

A single passion flower,
Focus.
Vital,
Organic,
It endures
The external assaults
Of rain,
Secret wind,
Pieces of dust,
And pebbles,
The parched earth.
It weeps its own tears
And renews itself,
Water only flows like champagne.
Water is wasted from floods,
The flower drinks
And shuns the overflow.
Its buds are never too wet
And never too dry.
It endures.
Surviving again the chaos
And the poison.
And I am the one who escaped
The undercurrent of the ash.

The Archangel Michael

May 21, 2013

The sacred
Archangel Michael
Symbolization of "who is like God"
Revealed
In the Book of Daniel
Three times.
He preserved me
I am beyond harm.
My lover likens me
To a shaman;
He changed his calling
I was an advocate
For those who are diseased
He praises me
Because my intuition
Envisioned an elixir
Now, he heals the wounded,
I am in awe
Devoted to the lares and penates,
I rarely leave my spiritual home,
My portfolio is sacred
Ensconced in my attic.
I draw heaven and earth
With the shadows of charcoals.
And poetry is couched in my soul.
When I am unsound,
I ponder on my Archangel Michael,
A miracle,

Full-bodied feathered wings
Evolve from my shoulder blades,
Flying to the music of the carillon bells
At The Botanic Gardens.
I sing a Gregorian chant.

A Silken Cream Ribbon

May 27, 2013

You always hid in the closet,
Away from the breaking dishes,
The screams,
The suffering,
Are you at peace now?
How is your sleep?
I will erase your scars.
A silken cream ribbon binds us together,
The ribbon is tied to my finger,
I tie the other end to your finger.
Remember that you are with me,
You are not *there!*
You wander all over the globe,
Running away
From your memories;
Stay home with me!!!
My long hair
Surrounds you
Like a pleated shade,
As I kiss you,
My pink lipstick
Is scented aloe vera
You are distracted
You begin to enter
Into the realm of
The meditation of our pressed lips,
You are now deeply into your breath,
And, then, into my body.

The Vault Of Heaven

June 6, 2013

The vault of heaven,
Flows downward
Like my red tulips
Falling like a dance,
An arabesque
Floating in space.
An adagio
As a man caresses
The woman,
And lifts her
Seamlessly;
She drapes over his shoulders.
She performs a pirouette,
Turning effortlessly
Around and around
Defying gravity.
The soul of the dance
Shapes her internal vision.
The vault of heaven
Flows downward.

Vapors

June 7, 2013

Ice
In a lustrous goblet,
Like steams of tears.
It binds my grief
Glazed with frost.
I am listless,
The rhythm of time
Suppresses the movement
Of the sun,
I cannot be washed away
By the vapors
Of a rivulet
That never thaws.
The glacial water
Cools my white shadow,
My swollen lids becalm
My desperation.

The Stillness Of A Zephyr

June 7, 2013

The grove and thicket
Defy the full-shock
Of the wind.
They cluster;
Their purple and yellow flowers
Are tearing away at their limbs;
The stillness of a zephyr,
Replaces the brutal heat-wind.
The savage wild
Transposes into a diminished force
Relaxing the thinning leaves.
The fruit still clings.
I clear the clutter
Of my refuge;
As I place a sheath
Upon the mud-stained ground,
I open a basket filled with corn bread
Surrounded by a thistle.
Then, I recall the tiny hummingbird,
Eating the enriched food
As his heart no longer rapidly flutters.

A Daily Haze

June 11, 2013

Supine
Listless
Quiescent on her chaise lounge;
Like a savant reading tomes,
And novellas
Of another soul's
Ability to replenish
Her dreams.
She is deceptive
Absolving
Her enrichment programs.
She states that she
Has a physical affliction.
Yet, often, cancels
Her piano lesson
Or her teaching-hours
Where she rejoices.
Her mendacity
Protects her from the
True crippling
Of her mind,
She is not ambulatory.
She imbibes cups of latte
And espresso or Kona coffee.
If only the caffeine
Would burst into vitality;
She attempts to awaken
Three hours

Before her commitment.
She remains in a daily haze.
She is dissolving.
Each day is a hurdle.
Her fetal position,
Subsumed under her yellow and green duvet.

Precious Honey

June 23, 2013

I sit on a large tree stump
Here, I have precious honey for you.
To sweeten the moment.
You are seated against a boulder,
I offer you a white porcelain bowl,
Filled with cherries and yams.
The sweetness cuts through
Caustic words.
A slight rose-bird warbles
In harmony with
Another feathered creature.
Vexation only lasts a few moments;
And, then polyphony.
Cumulus clouds
Sharing their symmetry,
As we sustain,
In the sylvan shade
My native words,
And your equilibrium
That tastes like malt sugar.

The Oblong Mirror

June 27, 2013

The oblong mirror,
Reflects haunted russet eyes,
A bindi,
A bright dot of red between my brows,
The third eye,
The sixth chakra,
Kundalini energy.
An aged Cuzco decorative vase
A cluster of fuchsia
And Sweet William,
A damask rose,
A book of Bengali text
Reading Hindustan
The flow of my sari,
As I prepare green tea,
And a curried dish;
The glare formulates
My metamorphosis
As a woman from the Eastern world;
The wind flutters
My white watered-silk curtains.

The Cracked Stone Wall

June 28, 2013

The cracked stone wall,
Wild the bird.
A rabbit is enclosed,
Where is the door?
I lay bleeding,
I am numb,
The rabbit nuzzles my arm,
Its fur,
Smells like sweet apples,
My leg,
Cut from the window pane.
I rushed in too quickly.
The bird sheds a feather,
It lands with the stillness of yarrow.
She shrieks,
The rabbit lies on my wound
Like a tourniquet,
The bleeding refrains,
Blue-cold and copper blood,
I search for heat,
The rabbit's breath,
A wisp of warmth.

A Wounded Wing

July 7, 2013

A severed wing,
"Here sweetheart,"
Sit in my palm"
She flutters
White dust,
Her eyes seals against the wind's suddenness of flight.
Now wasted,
She remains tranquil,
Her tiny heart
Is in cadence with the tide.
I shudder
At my own wounded wing,
An interior quest,
A severed blossom,
Birds shape themselves
Into the crust of the bark,
The leaves fall,
A protective cloak,
Camouflage.
My infusion of an herbal potion,
A Chinese brew.
Hesitantly, she drinks
From earthenware.
She deserves Limoges,
The cup that cheers.
Her nature is the flavor of honey,
I bond with her.

Psychic

July 8, 2013

White stucco,
An arched window,
Five-leaf ivy,
They are not parched,
The swirling liquid sunshine,
Our stone-clawed bench,
And Adirondack chairs
Of lime and cloud-blue,
Before the rush of rain.
Stargazers,
A herringbone,
Red brick patio,
I am second-sighted,
While in my meadow,
I can see within my telling dreams
The ocean foaming
Like impregnation
Or copulation,
It breathes new life.
And the drops of sweet-dew
Engulf me.

Red Rain

July 17, 2013

Red rain,
Dropping dandelion seeds,
Floating down
Into the moist soil,
Stuck,
Though I am blessed
As I retrace
My child, within
My womanliness.
Rewriting my past,
And longing for the
First breath of summer.
I walk barefoot
Into the clean moisture,
Clearing off the dead skin
On the bottom of my feet;
My nails are clear,
I will not paint them.
I prefer nature, unclothed,
Fallen velvet leaves
Surround and sun-dry my limbs.

The Forest-Flush Of Leaves

July 22, 2013

Swollen soil
Surrounding the Ginkgo tree,
The leaves are white
Spotted with mold.
My glass pitcher
Is filled with the red stain
Of healing food
Within the sparkling water,
I, too, have my own restrictions;
Starch and sugar
Poison me.
I consume sunflowers
And daisies,
And many greens
From the forest-flush of leaves;
The moon in mist,
The succulent leaves,
The wonder of dusk,
Yet dawn still weeps
With moisture,
The flavor of leaves;
The seasonings,
The herb-of-grace,
Thyme, savory, sage,
Chervil and cilantro.
Today, my blood is purified,
Like onions, clearing out the toxins.

I Am Mercurial

August 1, 2013

Mahogany doors,
An Alcove
A flush of candle-flame
On my drop-front desk
Papers strewn,
I lose words,
Their flight
Is my conception
I am not grounded,
I am mercurial,
Like a sea-bird
Lost in the green-hills,
I look for the wasted pond,
It is dry-dust,
The swarm of light-birds
Still searching,
And enigmatic
Like the words' pause,
The sentence leans,
Against my calligraphy
My handwriting slants
The wrong way.
My mind's eye turns to foam
As the water flows,
Floating away
Like my remote grasp
Of my pen's stain.

The Heart Of The Maze

August 6, 2013

A Chimera,
Leads me
Into a maze,
The base of the green wall
Vermilion leaves
My lover is courtly,
He respects my eremitic ways,
He awaits my composure.
When I seek the yellow ochre-colored bench,
Located in the heart
Of the maze,
I need to immerse myself,
While I write on rice-paper
The soft rustle
The whispering;
My frozen discernment,
Releasing the sweetness
Of my breath.
I wear a gossamer white dress,
Where my nipples
Are full,
Almost bare.
I wish to enter the bough
Uncloaked
Surrounded by the wonder,
The verdant calyx leaves.
A grounded bird
Lifts her wings

Cloistered

August 13, 2013

Night herons;
Sea-water
Sweet as currant wine;
I cannot lose you.
The white-brush
Of cirrus clouds,
Now opaque,
Swiftly stroke
Tears of ripples
Silently pulsing.
A small boat
Like a raft,
My oars pace
As the sea folds
Beneath the horizon
Braced for dusk;
You summon me.
I succumb to your call;
The loam-filled
Voluminous ridges
And surface-rocks
Pitch toward my boat,
A crescent shape;
I am cloistered
Without you.

I Sooth Sentient Beings

August 16, 2013

The day,
Is frozen
By the wand of a muse,
Calliope.
The torrent
Spills on my meadow
Yet preserves my gables and chimney—
My complete domicile.
The sun
Whitens the leaves.
The roots
Swallow the fathomless clay.
A Shard of stones
Break open the wounded cracked earth
As the water penetrates the summer-tree,
Their silver limbs
Droop;
A feral cat bounds onto my translucent sheath.
I tremble,
He purrs,
His fur ripples,
A cat's-eyes shift.
I experience solace.
I am solitary and unobtrusive;
I sooth sentient beings
With my lute.
I stow a bucket
Under the seeping tree's blossom.
I drink rain-water;
As rhubarbs feed shedding creatures during the first light.

Tibetan Prayer Beads

August 17, 2013

I stain my lips,
With blush-rose rouge.
A butterfly kiss
Is potent
While we share
The feather-bed,
Where birds flocked.
We enfold,
As I respire
As you caress my breasts
I wear a talisman,
A bracelet,
Two strands
Of Tibetan prayer beads.
My vow,
Your silver band,
Implies immortality
My long triangular chestnut hair
Evokes silken threads
That permeates your senses.
My subtle fragrance, attar of roses, is aromatic
And distilled
With an essential oil.
Our room is blessed by Aphrodite.
The oak-wood beams
A vaulted ceiling
The skylights
Reveal the eye of heaven
I am a priestess
And a sorcerer,
My amulet is placed
In a heart-shaped receptacle.

Utopia

August 25, 2013

If my spirit returns again,
To the earth's vastness
Envisaged
And nurtured
By the wisdom
Of designated seers
Who share their enigmatic secrets
At a Montessori school;
Or an esoteric tutor
Blends the rich mixture
Of the seasons of music,
Visionary art and poetry;
Songs and fables,
The mythology of Orpheus and Eurydice,
Daphne and Apollo,
My pictorialization would morph into a laurel bush.
A world without desks and walls;
Only bentwood rockers and wing-chairs.
And the exploration of nature's creations.
Trees bend and plead,
They, too, need a human touch.
The esplanade entices me;
I float within a hydrofoil
In the city of rivers.
Bound literature
Is stored in my valise;
My gurus
Follow my dream of utopia.

Shattered

October 18, 2013

Swept away
She roamed
The barren path,
The streets of the ruined slums
Seeking a screen from danger.
She fled brutality and oppression
From her kin and their filthy tenement.
Where was a foster home?
The Night-Ministry
Espied her huddled with white lips
As she burnt with fever and hallucinations—
Cadaverous,
Dying on the cold planks—
Dust motes floating
In a dilapidated concrete building
With needles, used condoms, mold and seepage,
Water like tears now pasted on her face.
Their white van
Retrieved her hollow shell.
Now, with a spacious room
She slept under the duvet covers,
And cleanliness permeated
The walls and floors,
As she was fed intravenously.
A bounty of books
Shared her space.
She was an autodidact.
Philosophical thoughts were valued

As was a Socratic education,
She began to cope in the interior
And the outer aspect.
Her endeavors led to her own bookstore
Attentive to authors' passionate symbols
And metaphors
In the sunlight of their prose.
A used piano—
Improvisation and harmony.
Her nest was a small artistic house—watercolors
And a stained glass window.
She flourished within her fertile patch—forsythia, dahlias and
gladiolus.
She shed her sorrow
And bonded
With her Burmese cat.

A Sylvan Cottage

October 26, 2013

Shattered glass;
Nervous, shaky,
Her tremor in both hands.
Her father—foreboding,
"Quit school at sixteen,
Bring home money.
The arts are worthless."
She resists him,
Still, her face
Is distended—
A purplish contusion.
She does not comply.
Her open university bestows tutors.
She is an apprentice to a librarian.
Writing is a tunnel, a focus,
A breath of an angel who is a seer.
She sustains her own sylvan cottage,
A loft for built-in bookcases,
She rereads Virginia Woolf's *A Room Of Her Own*,
And the poetry of Emily Dickinson.
In her breakfast room
She samples sage, ginger, and cardamom
Over baked salmon
She inhabits her living room
Where the fireplace haunts
Her, then releases luminosity
Throughout the diurnal dark period.

Her trestle table soothes her
With a bayberry candle
And two talismans—a frosted and etched butterfly and dragonfly.
She, too, was in flight
The dining room is for partaking sustenance
With her special lover,
Who is sagacious and contemplative,
She unearths his knowledge,
He is of an earlier vintage;
She is his help-mate, his comfort,
He ponders with his analytic mind in her sunroom,
On his drop-front desk.
She has her own book-lined niche where she sheds her past.
She is mystified by the quiescent space in her soul.
Within the secrecy of her dreams
While sleeping under her quilted bed
They are attuned to each other's essence,
They fondle, embrace and are secure in their intimacy.
Throughout her nest, her bow windows and skylights are plenty.
Her and his sunroom thrives with a bonsai tree, begonias, violets
and basil.
Baroque and Romantic music is meditation in motion,
The white and black keys of her piano
Interacts with his memories of the distance of the farthest star.

Vanished

November 4, 2013

Shanti, born in Bangalore;
Praying to the cruel goddesses
In the holy city—Banares.
She dreamt of her vows of
Her arranged marriage.
Her dowry was extensive
Or she would be shunned,
Yet she was violated—
Her defloration
Was by her father.
Her hymen was not intact.
She hid the heart's blood
Of a pig
In her leather pouch
For that dreaded night.
She had no beloved;
Yielding only to her husband
And mother-in-law.
Each night she would prepare his feast:
Bake, blanch, marinate and steep
While she wept.
Bear a son
Or abort a girl.
She was in pain
Because of her laceration and amputation of her clitoris
With broken glass
During her pubescent innocence.
She envied women

Who would slip away
And find their calling;
She hoarded books
Secret treasures of wisdom.
She was unwell
Because of fistulas
Due to genital mutilation.
She could not go to a man of medicine
Because he would find her wanting.
She was not a virgin.
She traveled to the end of the earth
And vanished.

The Silence Of The Soul

November 4, 2013

Desolate
When they are apart
A grim visage
She travails
Through Time;
Her body shifting
As she slips onto
Her chaise lounge
Within her refuge
Of her quill and her ink.
She attempts correspondence
With her astral lover.
Is distance evolution?
The propagation
Of the species is an epilogue
Human contact is extinct.
They cannot share their cerebral
And spiritual gifts.
Opulence and pieces of gold was his only answer.
She is interdependent;
She is his Geisha
And Aphrodite
Her nurturing is rebuffed,
Massage and fondling is an unheeded caress.
Music an intrusion.
Literature is slighted.
Sensuality is malignant.
She feels ruined;
She was not meant for the silence of the soul.

The Orchid

November 5, 2013

Obsession
And inquietude
A fragile orchid rarely survives.
The uncertainty of symbiosis;
Moss on a boulder
Is luminous.
Her wounded mother
With jumbled words,
Her clutter of language
The daughter was not spared;
She knew the code;
Words as hallucinatory symbols.
Her boundaries were brittle.
There were no tutors.
She was rebuffed
By the house of learning
She unearthed her books;
No time; no time
The utter waste;
She could not subtract,
Multiply or divide.
She was spatially challenged;
There was no nature or nurture.
She was the algae,
Or a single cell;
She did not transgress.
She bled throughout a spasm;
She bled beyond menstruation;

She feared poverty and pregnancy.
Her mother's tears—
So sad; So sad.
They entered the dark tunnel together, as one.

Earthly Garden

November 6, 2012

Daylight receding
In the early dusk,
The house of many windows,
Bereft of light.
Somberness dampens my psyche.
The blue ink
Permeates my chambers;
My soul recedes in a haze
Of deep dread and affliction.
So I illuminate my alcove
And all the shadows vanish.
The electric sun-charged pulsing rooms
Surprise my tulips
As they open in a sudden shock.
My gardenias bloom
Embracing the false sun.
I cannot conserve my habitat,
On my earthly garden,
My terrestrial sphere.

The Planetary Realm

November 8, 2013

No matter
How bleak and denuded
Is our planet
On the trespass of my senses;
I find the sensuality
Of brewing an herbal tea,
The healing chamomile liquid in my bone-china cup;
Or brushing honey-mustard glaze
On my baked poultry
The fragrance of wine
Simmering—
Coq au vin
Or scooping my acorn squash
When I dine alone
My endorphins elevate.
My plants are full and vivid
I wish to share my creations with my lover
Who is surrounding the secret rings of Saturn.
Nebula for Lyra,
Floating
The universe nurtures him
The traveling Dutchman,
The sense of the stars,
The astral body and the quasar.
The utter stillness of the universe,
Galactic vapor
The cluster of clouds and debris,
Creating laser-light

Onto the elements.
My cosmos,
My light clusters
Are a prism of rose glass, pastels, and the druids
Present in my sacred wood dwelling
My illuminated manuscripts,
An interior world.
In my dreams,
I visit you in your planetary realm.

The Persian Queen

November 11, 2013

A pregnant teenage girl,
Bereft
Is scorned
Her life skills spoiled
By her parents' culture and cruelty.
Except for her secret treasure
The proficiency in reading precious books.
She begs, forlorn in the muddy streets
Not spared the ghastly rubble, death.
Soon she is blessed
To discover an elderly blind woman
Who pays her a stipend
Bestowing her with an enchanting room
With built-in bookcases,
Reproductions of Monet, Renoir,
A pink-laced bassinet for her future child.
The girl creates stories
Decoding, translating books
Also meant for her daughter.
To this wondrous woman,
Who dwells in a Victorian house.
She reads the miracle of Queen Scheherazade's
"One Thousand and One Nights"
Where the queen creates awe
From her memories of poetry, philosophy, arts,
From her hollowed breath to the brutal Persian King, Shahryar
Who murdered all his former wives.
She relates antique races
Beguiling him.

After absorbing years
Of her tales.
She is his muse.
The Queen reflects, transmitting
The dreams of myths,
King Shahryar is besotted
By his queen, sparing her life.
The girl's daughter
Will spill words through the interior world of books
And will illuminate them
Throughout her precious life.
Her daughter dreams of her own small palace,
She is not forsaken.

The Triangle

November 11, 2013

Singing rocks,
The flowers tremble;
Days of wonder;
The tree's limbs bow
To the atonal music.
Crystals lie beneath the cave,
They hum.
All of nature vibrates;
The pitch is high;
We cannot detect sound.
I place a triangle
In the midst of the rocks
And the lush falling leaves;
I strike the cool metal,
A hummingbird flies
Toward the unnatural sounds;
She hovers over the instrument,
Her wings intensify the music.
In the silence of the forest,
All nature sings.

Karoshi (Sudden Death)

November 13, 2013

Consumed
Overstrained
He awakens before
The summoning of the dawn.
The down-wings of the birds,
Still in slumber;
He is overwhelmed,
Worsted;
Strained and exhausted,
His dreams are fragments
Totems of necrosis.
He is despondent,
Weary and trembling;
I sustain him;
With precious oils.
Lavender is tranquil;
He is in repose;
Unending childhood chores;
Affection was not even a word;
Reverie, fantasy, music, poetry and inner-vision
Were not permissible;
Neglect was fostered within his soul;
He wanders like a vine,
The tendrils grip him.
But I am his house-dweller;
He, now, summons my daydreams.

The Language Of Darkness

November 20, 2013

The daughter was the apprentice
Of the Language of Darkness—
As if in a foster home or orphanage;
Estranged from guidance, a tutor, or a school.
A vulnerable sacrifice.
She was her mother's heartfelt healer,
A curator of her mother's art of subjugation
And guilt.
Her mother's demented and delusional lesions
As pus
Void of a scab.
The fluid leaks,
There is no coagulation
It may as well have been the leaching of her blood.
No one
In this earthly vision
Sustained her
How could she persevere?
She might shatter.
The mother controlled her free-will.
Refusing her one friend.
The daughter poured her passion in the shape of her design.
Within her few classes
She was in a haze—
Hallucinations,
Words and vision distorted
The daughter barely endured the harrowing experience of loss of self,
A mirage.
Her body lingered in the firmament.

Safety

November 25, 2013

I was born on the losing side,
I represent the feminine,
With an unsound mind,
My God is not revered;
A pernicious family,
No money,
The loss of my tutelage.
It is an absurdity
That I can nurture myself;
But I do,
"I am safe"
I am nourished, sheltered
And cherished.
Though not by my own means.
Except through my/his creation,
The architecture of my soul,
The house of light and wood.
My abundance of bookshelves;
My private library;
I have come into my own,
I write my thesis,
Dwelling on my wandering,
Random dreams and words
Exploring the passionate
Letters "A to Z"
The phrases,
I burst like a ashen mum,
I am your flower of birth and death,
Speaking precious words of the spirit, the deities

And mysticism.
I long for your presence,
I am a keeper of tales, both dark and light
I heal you
I am your enigma.

The Runes

November 26, 2013

She perceives
The blush of a rainbow;
Preternatural,
She peers
At the cheval glass,
Inviting
This spectral visitant
To envelop her.
A solar shine
Awakens the day;
She lives in the moment;
She dismisses her genealogy;
She gathers
Ancient runes
For lucidity.
She lisps, overflowing
With the breath of lingual roots;
Evocative chants
Unveil her intuition;
She belongs to the firmament.
The runes are her orators.

A Fairy Staff

November 29, 2013

A foster home,
The mother
Who shines starlight,
The child's ribbons
Bloom outward
Like a satin heart.
"She no longer
Has to suffer.
Her eyes
Like the eastern sand,
Her dress
Like a diminutive gown
Of the goddess Parvati.
She is amenable
To the light-force of the mind.
There is no more flight,
Her satin ballet slippers,
Toe pointed
From sinewy long legs;
Her patrician and scholarly foster-father,
Bestows her a fairy staff,
His love never warps
In the dark.
Her nightmares are dissipated.

Sequestered

December 2, 2013

His family
Is misogynistic.
She should not succeed
Never an hour in the sun;
She cannot be her lover's co-equal.
She should propagate.
Abide in the scullery.
Every missive and gift
Has, only, his name.
She does not exist.
Culture is corrupt,
The arts are consigned
To the lower regions;
She feels like Persephone
Dwelling with the god, Hades.
She cannot be fruitful;
Only in the spring,
When the blush
And the still green glow
Reflects her mother, Demeter.
Yet, Persephone is in a passive state.
She has no spirit
To descry her own glory
Her ethereal longings
To create with her own blood,
Leaking from her delicate fingers,
Sonnets, couplets, alliterative
And pastoral verse

Or introspection.
She should comply with her lover;
She should not postulate;
She paints the northern lights
With her rainbow of illusion.
She is in her own space,
Her sequestered room has her silver key.

The Cold Estuary

December 3, 2013

She leaps and anoints herself into the cold estuary.
Her singular ritual.
Her frigid death-white dress clings to her skin;
Water drips
Her breasts revealed;
She hides behind
A bare lavender bush.
A stone-clawed bench
Beckons her;
She reclines.
She discarded her cape,
Even though the elements are raw.
There are no sun-parched clothes;
Clouds are masked by the gaunt
Shadows of the woods' tree-limbs,
The leaves shape themselves,
Surrounding her bare feet,
Ground-fed,
Waiting for spring.
She pours the ashes,
Clogged within the urn
Over the silent winter-grey;
She releases
Her childhood angst;
Tears are embedded
In her icy cheeks,
They drop like stolen flower buds,
Yet are translucent.
She bids her mother adieu;
Oblivion is just an illusion.

No Memory

December 4, 2013

It haunts me;
My lost memories;
Sleeping between my parents
Molested, a vague mist.
My father a terror.
Shrieked at me
"Quit school
At 16-years-old
And get a menial job."
No skills.
Locked me out—told me to become a prostitute.
An air mattress;
Sojourned at other people's havens.
No memory
Then, home, attended mentally ill mother;
No school.
Interior learning.
Vision of only two pedagogues
In grammar school;
High school records
All incomplete.
How did I graduate?
No memory.
Learning disabilities;
Childhood hallucinations.
Pediatrician stated to mom
A necessity of a psychiatrist
I was eight years old.
She refused.

I suffer privation.
Persevered through the arts.
No memory.
Where was Child and Family Services?

Homage To Love

December 6, 2013

Voyage
Enduring Gaea
The terrain
Where lovers connect;
There is self-sacrifice,
Their life work
Should not shatter
Their homage to love,
Spiritual coupling,
Heartfelt nexus.
Love is subsistence
Consecrated bread
I would live without sustenance;
My flowers would wilt and
Their sweet sprung colors would perish.
Parched, lime water
Like blood,
Would spill throughout the sea.
An aftershock.

Traveling Through The Stratosphere

December 13, 2013

Sun spots
The birth of a star
My elixir
Of cardamom and tarragon
Restores me
Though my lover
Is traveling through
The stratosphere
I am at peace
As I pace the cluster
Of the plains.
Placing six faces of snow crystals
That surround me
Like a hexahedron
As I pursue the subtlety of
Six degrees wind weather.
His path diverges,
But I sign,
Like a deaf person,
To the creatures,
Who intuit
My nature.
The hummingbird,
And blue jay,
Sweeten the air
They warble,
Without betrayal.

Haunted

December 22, 2013

Haunted,
Visions evolved;
A child-world filled with
Strings of thoughts,
Vexed emotions;
Fragments of fire
Seized by the smoke,
Undulating.
A dusk that reigns;
My disability constrains
Migraines.
As I resolve
The enigma of my memories;
Dissolving
When I sense my lavender incense
And bayberry candles;
My focus is acute.
The child-self will not entwine me.
A soft ecru lace-drape
Flutters from the
Coldest of air;
I avow my mantra's warmth
And the driving breath's heat.
Encircling
Within my alcove.
I place two botanical vases
Of exotic green mums?
The violets bloom.

Are they dyed by my rare illusions.
I resist the weather's hold
On my wounds;
I betray my past;
That is my courage.

Earthly Rhythm

January 2, 2014

Snow fall;
The roofs, their summits
Are reaching like translucent clouds
Bursting and spaced earthbound.
The wind explodes,
Stars, shaping flakes
Sweep around my haven.
I am the guardian of my shelter
Casement windows
And the strength of stucco.
A bunny warps the pristine white meadow,
His footprints break the silence;
I bend to the flutter of life;
The birds hide.
You place a white-gold ring
With tiny sapphires on my finger.
I wear it as a wedding ring;
You are endearing.
I am winsome.
My Peruvian ponchos,
Green Irish capes,
And multicolored shawls,

Flush me while I
Depart from my hearth;
I, also, meditate
On my fireside.
My grandfather clock
Chimes each precious
Earthly rhythm of the tide.
Yet, time is languorous
With each toll.
I espy a chimera;
I flow with this delusion;
She encompasses my form with her wings.
I know that I am unscathed
Each day is transient.
But I am not disposed to quietus;
I am not ready for the Hall of Souls.

The Allegory

January 7, 2014

The allegory
That sleeps in my inner surface-self.
The suppression of my words;
The stillness of the eternal night
Memories haunt me;
Solace
In sparing my life
And forsaking my symbolic death,
Buried in snow,
Hypothermia.
The green treasures
In my sun room;
Plants thick with leaves;
Flowers ferment
In their loam.
The thick partition
In my stucco house
Repress my cries;
The ice is jagged
The sweet waterfowl
Still chant
Breathing their songs
Of traveling and flight,
Magic and night,
Like a duck
They are corpulent
Invulnerable from the frozen tempest.
The gull

Is dense with the elements.
He is not fazed by the black ice.
He slides without variation
Toward the eastern loch.
Bats languish in their caves;
Bears hibernate from the tenuous light
A black swan, a rarity,
The temperate air breathes under my eaves;
Birds transport our spirits
Aloft;
The surface—a prism of a silken rainbow,
The texture of satin
Where there is no nebula,
Or cirrus clouds.
But I am sought
The birds have prolific seasons;
They weather-proof their nests.
The pine-needles never shed
Their light and dark green webs
Of leaves;
My heart is stolen
In late January,
The month of my birth.
I was born in a blizzard;
I am alive in winter
When I retreat
Within my words and my secrets
My wooden entrance-door does not warp
From the frost.

The White-Bird Of Mourning

January 13, 2014

Soft feathers drift,
A dim sky,
The sandpiper and the thrush
Do not despair;
The ruts are full,
I can sink into their depth
Like quicksand;
The funeral of your father,
His ashes,
His remains are not all burnt,
There is bone,
He does not vanish.
Your desolation
Is constrained.
The orb of night, Luna,
Will clarify
And usher in the evensong;
Wordsworth's poem
Is your prayer.
It focuses
On the apparition of the firmament
A white-bird of mourning
Ensues you.
The vault repels you.
There is no sweet scent
Of soil and clay,
Or flowers' roots
Embracing the heart of the dead;

Water and tears
Will not blend with peat moss and Gaea
The succulent leaves
Will leave no stain.
Grass will not shelter
With its green garb.
You fear coalescence
With his visitations.
Your angst
Consumes you.
You shun your ire.
Your visceral response
Confuses you.
I am here,
You are shielded
You are sacred
Within my psyche.

Linguistics

January 24, 2014

I am revealed through words
My syntax is singular,
You misinterpret me;
I feel like a misplaced person,
Strange and mystifying,
Your words are successive,
Threadlike.
I choose my books intuitively;
I impart my verbal allegories
To dazzle you
With my varied insights;
You are censorious,
Am I medusa?
My vision endangers you?
I am your terrestrial sphere;
Your world grasps your perceptions;
So I am obtuse,
My expressions are disorganized
Yet visual
Pre-Raphaelites are my language;
Linguistics are varied
I know the language of flowers;
The firebird is my dance,
The green tundra surrounds me
My fireplace glistens
I spark the flame;
Love lingers more than a moment;

Divine decree,
I am inquisitive,
I am your culvert,
Cuneiform, style
I connect with concertos
And harpsichords;
I am only your true convert.
I am your metamorphosis.

A Mist

February 1, 2014

A doe
Reclined in my meadow,
Supple,
I stroked her;
She typified tenderness
She was bountiful
She was enveloped
With pale flower buds
Blown down on my fingers;
My ringlets brushed her essence.
She is vulnerable
To human predators;
So am I,
I am delicate and raw;
I often retreat within my acres;
My sanctuary is my shell.
I fear the cluster of humanity.
The confluence of harsh discourse.
I speak in belles-lettres
And liturgical words;
I connect with a flower-burst;
The white lily and the pink orchid;
I am a shadow
Surfacing the world
In society;
I am lost outside my fence.
I am nebulous.
Only I retrieve the doe;

We grasp each others wounds;
I fear the bow and arrow;
She fears the weaponry.
My images are perishable;
As I personify shapelessness
I am but a mist;
I am not visible.

The Cobblestone Road

February 3, 2014

The clouds
Seize the sun;
It filters
Through the season's snow.
I search for you
Down the cobblestone road.
The sidewalks are muffled
With icy mounds.
The train's whistle
Is mute;
The cold wind
Does not carry an echo.
I contemplate the silence.
I behold you.
My eyes soften,
My heartbeat decelerates;
My panic erases
My tremor.
I breathe in the frost.
My deep rooted trepidation
Is abated.
I run toward you.
I am the vestige of your creation;
I present you
With my ceramic pitcher
Of hot chamomile tea.
At our sanctuary,
I rub your feet

And overlay your being with fleece.
The bay window
soothes the source of light;
Music releases your weariness.
I gather my roses
And translate my stolen words
From a book.
You like *The Dubliners* by James Joyce.
I glow
And transmit my substance.
My piano sings.

A Serum

February 6, 2014

The soil seeps
Blood-like;
A serum mimicking menstruation,
A time of sustenance.
It is celebratory,
It is pure.
Fertility is implied
Though I chose not to procreate.
It envelops my sex.
I am the essence of femininity,
Womanly,
The yin,
Softness
And flowers
My sachet and rose water
My spun-out tresses.
I embellish myself with a droplet of lustrous ornamentation—
Your eternal ring
My kaftans,
And sari
And my shimmering sheath.
I am the spirit of my house;
My hanging and floating gardens
Entwine the wandering vine;
I am in tune with the wild things
And my golden spotted feline;
I am intuitive

I appease you when you are pensive;
You are a voyager;
I am submersed in my folio
And my chromatic scale.
Flowers rush into bloom.

The Key

February 7, 2014

A house,
Locked,
The silver key glistens;
It releases
The pressure
Of the oak door;
A house,
Open
Welcomes the priestess
With her incense
And hot stone massages.
A medicine ball
Imbued with lavender,
An essential oil.
She waivers;
Her shadow rebuffs' her confidence.
Can she heal?
Whispers
Behind the Japanese screen,
She is bereft
Without her vocation.
She helps souls
Travel throughout their realm.
Her love
Toils at his calling.
He occupies
His own interior retreat
Near her unique shrine.

Their space enhances their ardor.
They share sustenance
At dawn and dusk.
He enters her,
The cadence of their hearts.

The Eucalyptus Tree

February 14, 2014

I perceive snow caves,
I think of igloos
And hibernation;
The ice-mounds tilt,
They can collapse
I walk toward the woman
Carrying flowers in her basket;
She is hidden and warm
In her portal,
The multi-colored day-flowers
Resist the cold,
They do not whither;
Their buds are full and open
She is a vagabond,
Carriages lapse;
How will she
Return to her domicile?
Maybe a homeless shelter.
I relinquish my coins;
The scent of lilies is genitive;
My new fragrance,
Emanating throughout my crucial points:
The wind exhales.
I yield my flowers to my lover.
We had an assignation;
Meeting in the woodlands.
The glazed ice glistened,
We will converge under the depths
Of the eucalyptus tree.

A Gypsy

February 14, 2014

When we first met
The night startled
Our caress,
Who are you?
Who am I?
We were blessed;
You dreamt of poetry,
I sought your psyche;
My pages were creased
With misuse.
Your past was empty;
My past was replete with memory;
You surpassed me.
Balance was never in duration.
My hands cupped a firefly;
I released it.
You thought I was a seer
Who created pottery.
And macramé.
My piano startled you,
As did my flute.
We spared our separate souls;
Then we intertwined;
You traveled an odyssey;
My world of color and the senses.
Songs replete with imagery.
Your genius
And your force;

I wished I owned your office;
I had nothing but the four walls
And felt like a gypsy
In her caravan.
No space; a minute desk.
Our passage was turbulent.
I explored our new sanctuary,
My own alcove,
My treasure.

The Arms Of Morpheus II

February 16, 2014

I rest in the arms of Morpheus,
Heavily;
Deeply
I cannot gain consciousness
For twenty four hours.
Excessive work,
My vitality falters,
Fragile stamina,
I am not vigorous.
My eyes are distended
Flashes of awareness
Is ruined.
My waking life
Is extinguished.
My impairment
Where is my guardian?
My seraph
Ministering my spirit?

If I chant to Genesha,
The Hindu god who overcome obstacles
Maybe he will be bountiful
With psychic energy.
Caffeine is wasted,
As I am depleted.
I am a tutor;
I instill wisdom with words
And parchment.
I am earnest and bookish.
My spirit is forced down.
How can I compensate
For being incapacitated.
I am forced
To let go of my calling.
I shatter easily.
I revel in my work;
But my clock ceases to chime.
The pendulum's pause.
I need unbroken hours
For reflection.
My muse
Seeks my scattered words,
And Bach's "Musette,"
My chromatic chords.
I am mystified.

A Tutor

February 17, 2014

Keats was poor;
The Romantic poets
Were his guardians.
Emily was loved
And solvent;
Virginia's Leonard
Sought her psyche;
He was awestruck.
I do not have consumption
Only my own darkness—my own impairment.
But I travail.
I am enduring.
If only I had been a woman of letters;
Walking up the stairs
I am dazed by the height.
A small college
With collective wonder;
I am no longer a novice;
I would flourish
As an autodidact
And a bibliophile
The substance of enlightenment.
I am under the aegis of my lover;
I thrive in my manor,
My desk is unencumbered.
The snow crystals
And the sleet
Are perceived behind my transom.
My vocation encompasses
My severed soul.

Shelter

February 18, 2014

I am under the blue-green quilt
With multi-colored flowers,
I am depleted;
I ascended the snow hills,
Enraptured by the meteors of crystals,
My diminutive shovel
Forged a ring
Around my birch tree,
The base of the trunk's spine.
It shies from the large bird house;
I sketch an oriole and a finch
With charcoal.
I perceive a future pastel drawing
Of the blue jay.
White shifts
Of mounds,
Quaking the ill-formed ground.
A possum rubs against the bottom of my cape.
How can I warm the earth
Without spraining my wrist?
I find formed clay;
I feel like an archeologist;
It is chipped,
Yet, a mercurial yellow;
I yearn to throw pots;
A fragment of myself
Discovered before the end of time.

The Clouds

February 19, 2014

I descend the staircase
Into my first floor loft.
My lover is wayfaring.
I prune my plants in my sun room;
I am a nature goddess.
Sunshine beckons me.
Snow plummets,
Sliding on my roof.
Ice is imprecise.
My window is blinded.
It cracked;
Water seeps intermittently;
Trespass;
Easily it seals.
I protect my resources
Both psychic and environmental.
I am revealed in my lover's office
Separated by French doors.
Here, I am invulnerable
And safe-guarded.
I still perceive his presence.
My spacious cottage
Awaits him.
My voyager skims the clouds
and the hue cycle.

Visions

February 21, 2014

The wind crushes against
The stucco;
The plain leaves rupture
The frozen cypress tree;
The meadow is fallow;
The roads weave
Into a cul-de-sac
Like a floe;
The point of my compass
Is obscure.
I am spatially challenged.
I will not abandon my acreage
And seek adversity;
A meadowlark has a crushed wing.
I place him in a receptacle;
The morrow I will
Seek a shaman;
I only use herbs
And spells
Though I am not a midwife.
I focus well in a theta state;
I soothe myself
Before I heal
Despondent creatures
My candles glow;
My mélange
Brews with deliberation.
Spices and herbs emanate
Their bouquet.

Afterwards, I perceive a mirage.
My visions are my calling.

Twilight

February 21, 2014

Clarion-voice sounds
Shatter me.
Incandescence blinds me.
Tempests bear down on me.
Pungent cayenne pepper poisons me.
Smoke fumes are rancid.
Yet all your
Senses beguile me.
For you, I press purple buds.
My orange flowers
Evoke the night,
My lips
Touch your lips,
I adorn myself,
I whisper throughout twilight,
You taste my salted tears
I breathe in your redolent skin like parchment.
My dreams entwine you;
Our love is other worldly;
Pietistic.
I stain my lips with berries;
I blush;
My eyes are an eclipse.
My silken ribbons
Clasp the small front braid
Of my hair.
It clings to you.

Empathy

February 28, 2014

Her eyes
The color of moonstone;
His, of slate;
She perfects the fireplace;
They whisper
Their secrets;
Concealed antiquity;
She places a cotton throw
On the floor.
Neither is culpable;
They absolve their fears;
The house is heavy
Against the wind.
They are shielded and nourished.
They dine
On brie and blueberries,
A glass of chardonnay.
She writes a novelette
Mythologizing their travails;
The flames respire their utterance;
They enfold,
Droplets down her cheeks;
She relates to his psychic pain;
A filament of her long tresses
Cascades over his shoulders,
They sigh.

Shifting Toward Harmony

March 10, 2014

Mirrors
Peer upon my aspect,
I drape
My shoulder-shawl
Surrounding
My susceptible
And shaky frame.
Emotionally,
I am shifting
Toward harmony.
I fear
That I will succumb
To desolation.
Yet I behold
The wearing of the trees,
Their sinews
When rebounding.
The shifting of the snow,
The new breath of green,
The floral envelope.
The shuddering wind
Risking the sweet spring.
The free-bird's new song,
The illuminated heath;
I dream of the moors on a windy day.

In Your Sorrow

March 11, 2014

I will do anything
To yield to you.
I will create an untraditional quiche;
And rouse before the sun
Serving you haute cuisine.
Mas La Barque Tapestry Coverlet
With bouquets,
Fleur-de-lis seal,
Archaic roses
On this spun
French tapestry
As I overlay your feet with alpaca.
I, your seer
Realize the abyss
Of your anguish
You are, now, an orphan.
Let us bereave in the throng of the supple woods;
Catalpa and ficus trees
You are sustained
In the meadow of the primrose and cyclamen.

Meteors

March 12, 2014

I string earth-beads,
Necklets and jade pendants.
When my mind is tremulous
I create ornaments,
I stumbled on secret planets' minerals,
From meteors and hidden caves.
Peru has sightings
Of oblong and glittering flying machines.
Mysterious craters
Banish signals.
And like an archeologist,
I espy their jewels;
A healing force
Draped around my neck.
Unknown creatures,
Shape-shift
They are unobtrusive mortals;
I await the tunnel of light
That blinks red;
The Sefert galaxy,
Quasi-stellar objects
Descend into my consciousness.
My beads are beacons.

Midnight

March 14, 2014

Midnight,
A flash of green;
White stars;
I curl up
In my blue chaise lounge;
I record your whispers
In my daybook;
I am a scribe.
I descry your dreams;
You are soaring
Above the pockets
Of clouds;
I am bursting
With your pictorializations,
Dadaistic imagery.
I peruse your psyche.
When the vapor darkens,
I enter into the intimacy of your reverie.
Now, you are moonstruck
And I fly with you
Into the dawn;
Nocturnal ruminations
I meliorate your soul.

Peril

March 16, 2014

A cranberry marsh,
Unsettled woodsman,
Aiming his gun
At precious yew-birds;
The gnarled tree
Blocks his vision;
I walk aimlessly;
I whisper to the ducks,
"Careful,
You are fraught with peril."
My muslin gown,
The color of cumulus clouds.
I am not color coded.
I don't even wear rouge;
My lips are light-pink.
The trunk of the tree
Blends with my blown russet locks.
I take flight,
Running back to my terrace.
I hear a gun fire like a missile,
I curl in the corner
Of my pantry,
In my wooden dwelling,
Crafted by the variation
Of trees surrounding me.
I heed his lust for slaughter.
I vow to survive
The chaos of our time.

The Virgin Meadow

March 17, 2014

The wind snaps the branches;
Once solid, a source for the birds;
The roots of the grass
Pressures green growth.
The naked tree
Releases its sap.
Feral cats
Sleep under the yew-tree.
Their nature
Is wild
And rampant.
The monthly cycle
Of female mammals,
They pace themselves
With a heavy gait.
The possum strides
Through my meadow.
I am wary;
There is no domestication.
The birds coalesce with their flock;
The seasons of the moon yield
The fruit of the night-fall.
The sun spots transform the climate;
The liquids in my body
Compensate
With the currents of the river.
River-rocks are stable
They smooth the path.

The cloud explodes,
The rain bursts
The waterfalls,
Like sudden foam.
The wheat fields are golden,
I am prostrate
In the center of the untilled wheat.
A virgin meadow.

Heather

March 18, 2014

You profess
You love my heather-filled moor.
I am lame without you.
A diurnal dark period;
The strain of enduring;
Our partaking of sage and turmeric;
You comprehend my scrolls;
I scrutinize your communion;
You drink from my tea urn;
I am your belletrist;
I am your interpreter;
I miss the press of our lips;
You envelop me.
Your voyage to remote lands;
I am bereft
And alone.
I obsess on your reemergence.
Like Othello
Your are wise;
I await your parables.
You are a legend.